D1389184

The Proper Care of
SNAKES

The Eurasian viper Vipera berus. *Photo: Dr. D. Terver, Nancy Aquarium, France.*

ARMIN GEUS

Facing page: An orange juvenile of the Emerald Tree Boa, Corallus caninus. *Photo: S. Kochetov.*

The Proper Care of
SNAKES

Armin Geus

Nose-on view of the Eastern Diamondback Rattlesnake, Crotalus adamanteus, *perhaps the most dangerous snake in North America. Photo: R. Everhart.*

CONTENTS

Snakes can be a colorful, decorative hobby if the keeper is willing to expend the time and money on the proper show cages and care. Photo: S. and H. Miller.

Introduction

There are all sorts of motives for keeping animals in the terrarium. However, the majority of people who bring amphibians or reptiles into their home would like to experience these living creatures (which usually lead clandestine lives and are still much maligned due to superstition, religious prejudices, and their supposed dangerousness) at close range, and would like to see and observe with their own eyes what they have read or heard about.

By fulfilling such wishes, however, they assume the responsibility not only for keeping the animals alive for as long as possible but also to make serious endeavors to provide optimal keeping conditions, to breed the animals, and to pass on what has been learned.

Anyone who has decided to keep snakes should not

allow himself/herself to be dissuaded, as long as the necessary containers and housing facilities are available. The keeper of boa constrictors, pythons, or anacondas obviously needs to have more space than that required for small, slender water snakes. The owner of poisonous snakes, in turn, must construct terraria which can be kept securely closed so that nothing untoward is liable to happen which might endanger him or his family. While the information a book of this scope can provide must confine itself to a few of the most important rudiments and fundamentals of snake-keeping, it is hoped that it will inspire the reptile lover to turn to the fairly extensive scientific literature and the standard works on terrarium management for the benefit of the pets in the keeper's care.

Normally cages for snakes are less finished and not designed for show. They should be utilitarian: roomy, secure, and easy to clean. Photo: R. W. Applegate.

Setting Up the Terrarium

The terrarium, in our case the snake terrarium, is as exacting with regard to its location and maintenance requirements as an aquarium. For the sake of the vegetation alone it must be placed in a location where there is plenty of light and where sunshine can enter. Although there are some snakes whose well-being does not depend on

A cage for a single snake or a small group of compatible snakes can be spartan but attractive. Cages sometimes are sold at pet shops and also can be located through mail order dealers. Photo: S. and H. Miller.

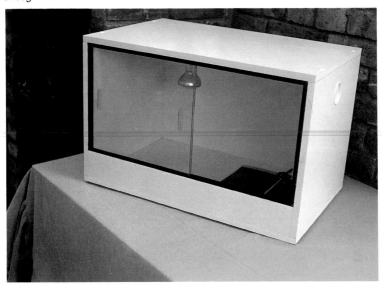

A paludarium or aqua-terrarium contains habitat for both terrestrial and aquatic animals. Arboreal (tree-dwelling) snakes often can be kept in the high humidity of such habitats. Photo: B. Kahl.

prolonged daily exposure to sunlight, light and sun nonetheless remain the elixir of life for the majority of reptiles. A window facing south or southeast would seem to be a suitable location. However, this must not be interpreted to mean that snakes need to spend the whole day, uninterruptedly, in a room flooded with light. It is perfectly in order for the cage to provide cool hiding places as well, which can easily be created by furnishing the container accordingly. Then the animals have free choice as to where they want to be. An accurate thermometer such as offered at pet shops enables the keeper to check the atmospheric temperature inside the terrarium at any time so it can be adjusted when necessary.

Ventilation should be given special attention, since it is a fact, where closed containers are concerned, that not only does the temperature rise quickly but also that the atmospheric humidity increases greatly. This latter has an adverse effect on the health of steppe- and desert-

Hiding places are very important for secretive animals like snakes. Both natural and manmade hides can be found at your pet dealer. Photo: W. B. Allen, Jr.

Efficient fiberglass cages are easy to clean and store, but they are too much like laboratory cages for the tastes of many keepers. Photo: W. B. Allen, Jr.

dwelling snakes and can lead to diseases of the respiratory passages.

An increase in humidity often occurs after the plants have been watered, as part of this water evaporates before it seeps into the sand. If the desired rise in humidity has not been achieved in this way, it will be sufficient to spray the terrarium with tepid water a few times.

Depending on the origin of the snakes, a heater of greater or lesser capacity will be required. This is essential where snakes from tropical countries are being kept, since their life cycle is rarely interrupted by hibernation. For heating the floor, there are plate- or box-shaped items on the market, with a step-by-step control of the wattage. These are watertight and can therefore be used for damp floor coverings as well. When installing such heaters there is no need to worry as to whether the bottom layer is receiving the same amount of heat everywhere. The inmates will very quickly find out where the warm places are and then seek them out regularly. Pliable lead pipe heaters, also watertight, can be installed not only in the aquatic area of an aquaterrarium for snakes but can be used to heat the atmosphere as well. In this case they need to be

A very simple but satisfactory cage setup for a 2-meter Pine Snake. Photo: W. B. Allen, Jr.

insulated with ornamental cork to prevent burns to the animals.

Another method to warm or heat the atmosphere is to use carbon-filament lamps as a source of heat. The carbon-filament lamp is fitted inside a hollow stem, again consisting of ornamental cork. The top end is closed off with wire gauze. The lamp can be conveniently hidden under suitably arranged ornaments to prevent the animals from entering the improvised heater.

To supplement natural daylight, but primarily to prolong the daily assimilating activity of the plants, it is advisable to work with economical fluorescent tubes which give a good light. When choosing the type of tube make sure the proportion of red in the spectrum of the lamp is not too large as this kind of light encourages vertical plant growth and leads to sickliness of the shoots.

The need for ultraviolet irradiation is best met by using appropriate lamps from your pet shop. Fifteen to 20 minutes of irradiation two to three times a week are perfectly adequate. Infrared lamps can be used in addition. These not only emit light-energy but also guarantee a considerable supply of heat.

For heating larger water tanks, such as those required in the terrarium, the appliances in normal commercial use are available in a wide range of wattages and designs. Glass tube heaters in particular are hygienic and easy to clean.

Those wanting to keep exotic snakes, regardless of where they originate, should decide on the species well in advance. Their needs then can be taken fully into consideration when the heaters are installed.

For water snakes a fairly spacious water basin is essential. Where the snakes

A New Guinea Green Tree Python, Chondropython viridis. *Such snakes are not for beginners.* Photo: B. Kahl.

go into the water only occasional-ly a small basin in which they can bathe (the size of a developing dish) is sufficient. This should be sunk in the sand to the rim. For the true water-loving species, on the other hand, such as the Ringed or Grass Snake *(Natrix natrix)* or the Tessell-ated Snake *(Natrix tessellata)*, a larger basin is recommended.

These water basins, whatever size or shape is required, can be modelled without difficulty from a mixture of coarse sand or gravel and cement (sand to cement = 1:2). After they have

Many snakes need access to bathing facilities if they are to be kept successfully. One such species is the Eurasian Grass Snake, Natrix natrix. *Photo: B. Kahl.*

set, however, they must be watered for three weeks, in running water if at all possible. Leaky spots if any, should be patched with cement or lined with paraffin. Around the edges of the water container the ground should be covered with coarse gravel so that the water displaced when

the snake leaves the container can seep away quickly.

Apart from snakes which live in extremely dry habitats, all species should have access to bathing facilities. Around the time when they shed their skin even those snakes regarded as wholly terrestrial go into the water.

For esthetic reasons the snake-keeper will strive to landscape his containers with bizarre tree trunks, branches covered with moss, and attractive plants. Pleasing the eye should not be the only reason for furnishing the terrarium with such objects, however. Rather, they should be arranged in such a way as to be of use to the snakes when they shed their skin.

Rough surfaces, pieces of bark, and narrow passages between stones make it considerably easier for them to strip off the old skin.

Among all groups of reptiles snakes lead the most secluded lives. This important prerequisite for normal behavior should be taken into account by providing a variety of hiding facilities (which it should be possible to check up on at all times). Suitable building materials for these hiding places are tubes of ornamental cork, larger stones which have hollows and lie flat, and tree trunks as well as their roots.

Snakes are able to move quickly not just on level ground. Most of them are agile climbers of trees and shrubs as well, the Aesculapian Snake *(Elaphe longissima)* being one example. Only the shorter, stockier species such as the Adder or Common European Viper *(Vipera berus)* find climbing difficult.

Depending on their habits, the snakes will require ample climbing facilities. Richly forked branches from elderberry trees are excellently suited for this purpose. Many keepers of tropical snakes—for instance, arboreal snakes of the genera *Atheris, Bothrops,* and *Lachesis*—like to attach various bromeliads and other epiphytes to the climbing branches. Some snakes, such as the true

thin body and sharp edges along the underside, actually move with far greater agility among the tree branches than they do on snakes, the ground. Particularly charact- where such nimble climbers erized by are being kept one must having a

make absolutely certain, therefore, that the terraria are securely closed and escape-proof everywhere, because their extremely flexible skeletal structure gives the snakes an amazing ability to get out through narrow cracks and

Although the rat snakes, genus Elaphe *do not look like arboreal snakes, many (such as this Aesculapian Snake,* Elaphe longissima*) are excellent climbers—and fine escape artists. Photo: B. Kahl.*

small openings.

To ensure the well-being of the terrarium occupants, proper cleaning of the containers is absolutely essential. Through cleanliness and care the occurrence of dangerous diseases is prevented. The glass windows are cleaned

with the aid of window-cleaning gadgets equipped with readily replaceable razor blades. To prevent the window glass from getting steamed up, which happens usually when there is a drop

Short, stocky snakes often find climbing difficult. Vipera berus, *a common Eurasian viper, seldom leaves the ground. Photo: B. Kahl.*

in the external temperature, it is advisable to apply a thin film of glycerine and water (in the ratio of 2:1) to the inside of the window. Food leftovers, dead plant particles, and feces (the latter often produced in considerable quantities by snakes) are best removed with broad wooden forceps. The water basin can be conveniently cleaned by siphoning off the water with a long rubber or plastic tube. Terraria which are in use all the year around need to be cleaned once a year. This includes replacing part or all of the bottom layer and thoroughly washing and brushing stones, roots, and rock constructions. Where the terraria are occupied only during the warm season the more thorough cleaning is most conveniently done when the animals have gone into hibernation.

In preparation for these tasks it is advisable to make sure that the animals get plenty of food, particularly in the late summer months, so that they have ample energy reserves to draw on during the lean winter months. Where native temperate species are concerned, the animals are best liberated in about September, either at the original collecting spot or in locations where food is especially abundant.

The simplest method is to use the terrarium itself as a hibernation container and to put it, complete with inmate, into a room that is cool and light but does not get frost (temperature about 4 to 6°C). If this form of wintering is not possible due to lack of suitable premises, the animals will have to get through the cold season in special hibernation containers. These should consist of firm wooden boxes with lids and holes (closed off with wire gauze) on two sides which allow the air to circulate.

The bottom of the box is

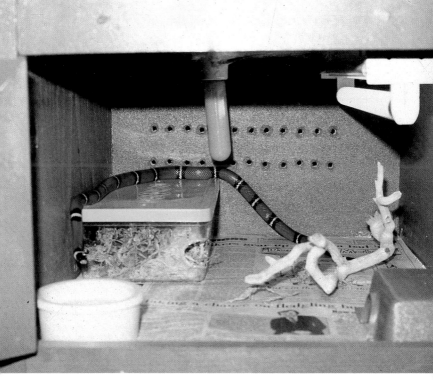

Many keepers like a cage that is efficient and easy to clean while providing everything the snake needs for comfort. Such cages seldom are landscaped to resemble natural habitat. Photo: J. Gee.

covered with a layer of moderately damp river sand (10 to 15 cm). On top of that goes a layer of sphagnum, dead leaves, or peat, damp but not wet and of the same depth. To stablilize the necessary atmospheric humidity during hibernation a shallow bowl of water can be placed inside the box. Securely closed, the winter quarters are then placed in a frost-proof, well-ventilated basement room. It is strongly recommended to check up at intervals of eight to fourteen days to be certain the litter is still damp. At the same time, any animals that have died must be removed immediately.

The end of hibernation is best left to the natural weather conditions. The animals wake up of their own accord and should then be moved back into the actual terrarium. It is an advantage to offer the snakes a tepid bath as soon as they are awake to initiate the removal of fecal remains from the proctodaeum. Hibernation starts at the beginning of October and continues until about the middle or end of March. In mountainous regions it may not come to an end until early May. To shorten the resting period, the container must not be brought straight from the cool cellar into a warm room. Rather, the "rousing" should proceed slowly by a gradual raising of the room temperature.

DRY SNAKE TERRARIA

It is when setting up a dry, unheated terrarium, suitable for keeping Adders *(Viper berus)*, Smooth Snakes *(Coronella austriaca)*, and Aesculapian Snakes *(Elaphe longissima)*, for example, that we are most likely to succeed in creating a natural habitat.

Let us suppose the objective is to mimic a small piece of heatherland or a sunny mountain slope. The bottom layer will consist mainly of coarse gravel; among the heather and blackberry runners we deposit angled stones. A moss-covered, gnarled tree trunk can make the picture look less stark and enhance the natural effect. In the background stand one or two little pines. To give more of an impression of a mountain slope, various pieces of the genus *Sedum* (stonecrop) will be planted in addition. Where there are Aesculapian Snakes *(Elaphe longissima)* in the terrarium, widely ramified and knee-high branches must not be absent.

A dry terrarium with moderate heating is suitable

Kingsnakes, such as this banded phase California Kingsnake, Lampropeltis getulus californiae, *can be kept in moderately dry, moderately warm terraria if given access to correct lighting and food. Photo: K. Lucas.*

Many snakes need quite dry terraria, especially species from deserts and dry savannahs. This Diadem Snake, Spalerosophis diadema*, from Israel is one such species. Photo: R. T. Zappalorti.*

for keeping all sorts of snakes from the Mediterranean countries, such as the Balkan Whip Snake *(Coluber gemonensis)*, the Horseshoe Snake *(Coluber hippocrepis)*, the Large Whip Snake *(Coluber jugularis)*, the Western Whip Snake *(Coluber viridiflavus)*, the Montpellier Snake *(Malpolon monspessulanus)*, the European Cat Snake *(Telescopus fallax)*, the Asp Viper *(Vipera aspis)*, and the Horned or Sand Viper *(Vipera ammodytes)*. If we stock the container with Mediterranean fauna, we will also need Mediterranean plants. Characteristic above all is the myrtle. Further, we use laurel, holly, oleander, small lemon trees, small fig trees, and box-tree.

If the snakes originate from the African steppes or from the Near East, then the terrarium must be adapted to the extremely dry regions which are often devoid of vegetation as well. Sand as fine as dust and stony ground cover the dry and hot earth. Under-floor heating is essential. Hardy Euphorbiaceae, *Cotyledon* species, and species of the genus *Caralluma* make up

the vegetation which, if cleverly arranged, can make the steppe motif look very pleasing. Suitable inhabitants are, for example, *Lytorhynchus diadema*, the Hissing Sand Snake *(Psammophis sibilans)*, and the sand boas of the genus *Eryx*.

For planting terraria intended to accommodate snakes from the dry regions of the New World, numerous cacti are at our disposal, although *Hechtia* and *Dyckia* species can also be

Many beginning hobbyists make the mistake of trying to keep water snakes such as this Nerodia erythrogaster *too moist, leading to fungal infections. Photo: W. B. Allen, Jr.*

employed. Sticks of *Yucca filamentosa* are particularly decorative. Of the snakes, only *Agkistrodon contortrix laticinctus*, a subspecies of the Copperhead, and other pit vipers such as *Crotalus cerastes* and *Crotalus viridis lutosus* shall be mentioned here.

MOIST SNAKE TERRARIA

Grass or Ringed Snakes *(Natrix natrix)* and, temporarily, Dice or Tessellated Snakes *(Natrix tessellata)* can be kept in the unheated, moist terrarium. Nevertheless, it is more favorable to accommodate them in an aquaterrarium for native snakes. How the heated, moist terraria are arranged and planted depends on the continents from which their inmates originated.

Typical plants of the humid African rain forests are the epiphytic mosses and ferns of which there is an abundance of species. Nonetheless, the wealth of epiphytic plants cannot match the rich variety of plants found in tropical America. The most striking species are the magnificent spleenworts *(Asplenium)* and the bizarrely lobed staghorn ferns *(Platycerium)*. For planting the bottom, we would recommend the species of the genera *Sansevera*, *Chlorophytum*, and *Dracaena*. Suitable occupants for terraria representing a section of African rain forests are the African species *Boaedon lineatus*, Jameson's Mamba *(Dendroaspis jamesonii)*, the Gaboon Viper *(Bitis gabonica)*, and the Rhinoceros Viper *(Bitis nasicornis)*.

If we wish to keep Asian forms such as the Indian Python *(Python molurus)*, the Blood Python *(Python curtus)*, the Reticulated

Facing page: A heavily planted tropical terrarium. Most snakes will simply disappear in such a terrarium. Photo: B. Kahl.

Python *(Python reticulatus)*, and the Mangrove Snake *(Boiga dendrophila)*, the plants we will be selecting to mimic their native landscape will consist of the famous and peculiar pitcher-plants *(Nepenthes* species), the climbing *Pothos* species, *Cissus discolor, Alocasia cuprea*, and the species of the genus *Aglaonema*, among many others.

There is an immense variety of plants that can be used when it comes to setting up a moist South American terrarium. Here the temperatures must never fall below 18°C, and the atmospheric humidity should be around 80 to 90%. Numerous ferns, Aaron's rod plant, and begonias serve as bottom vegetation. In addition, lianas such as *Medinilla, Vitis*, and climbing Leguminosae may be grown. Where epiphytic trees are concerned we have a particularly wide range to choose from. Members of the pineapple family (Bromeliaceae) such as *Bilbergia, Aechmea, Nidularia, Aregelia, Vriesia,* and *Tillandsia,* orchids, ferns, and cacti are represented by numerous epiphytic forms.

Only a few of the snakes suitable for these terraria shall be mentioned here: the Anaconda *(Eunectes murinus)*, the Boa Constrictor *(Boa constrictor)*, the Emerald Tree Boa *(Corallus caninus)*, and the various species of the genus *Bothrops.*

AQUATERRARIA FOR SNAKES

When setting up aquaterraria for snakes it must be decided whether they are to be communicating or non-communicating containers. In the former case, the bottom layer will constantly be saturated with water, which means the terrarium is in effect a humid one and

A Brown House Snake, Boaedon fuliginosus, *from southern Africa. This is one of the more adaptable species, surviving well under most terrarium conditions. Photo: G. Dingerkus.*

accordingly needs to be equipped with marsh plants. A less moist terrestrial area, on the other hand, which can be created by building in a shallow aquarium, can be stocked with plants that have lower water requirements. Animals for a European snake aquaterrarium are the Ringed or Grass Snake *(Natrix natrix)* and its various races and subspecies, the Dice or Tessellated Snake *(Natrix* tessellata), and the Viperine Snake (Natrix maura). Suitable plants are marsh marigolds (Caltha palustris), which grow on the edges of all stagnant or slow-flowing water, water plantain (Alisma plantago), arrowhead (Sagittaria sagittifolia), yellow iris (Iris pseudacorus), common sundew (Drosera rotundifolia), sweet-flag (Acorus calamus), bog arum (Calla palustris), branched bur-reed (Sparganium erectum), cranberry (Vaccinium oxycoccus), common butterwort (Pinguicula vulgaris), and various club-rushes or bulrushes (Scirpus). For the water container, use Canadian waterweed (Elodea canadiensis), lesser and greater bladderwort (Utricularia minor and Utricularia vulgaris), hornwort (Ceratophyllum), pondweeds (Potamogeton), and willow moss (Fontinalis antipyretica).

Among the exotic water snakes frequently kept are the Water Moccasin or Cottonmouth (Agkistrodon piscivorus), various members of the subfamily Homalopsinae, and North American Nerodia species. Among them are many dietary specialists which often accept only quite specific kinds of food animals. Fishes and batrachians are preferred to anything else.

COLLECTING AND SHIPPING SNAKES

After hibernation the snakes leave their winter quarters at the end of March if the weather is favorable. Resting in the warm spring sun, they are generally still lying in close proximity to their hiding places. Hence spring is the best time for collecting snakes, since they have not become very agile or particularly voracious as yet. In the summer, snake trapping can be successful particularly on days when it is humid and close and there is a thunderstorm brewing.

Actual catching is done by quickly taking hold of the snake with the hand, which should be protected with coarse leather gloves. Non-poisonous snakes, however, can be picked up with the bare hand without any qualms; the animals seldom bite seriously, most bites *(Elaphe* being a major exception) being just scratches. Far more of a nuisance are the unpleasant-smelling feces, excreted especially by Grass and Dice Snakes and garter and water snakes. The

A juvenile Rainbow Boa, Epicrates cenchria. *This gorgeous snake is one of the most attractive boids available and is fairly hardy in captivity. The beginning hobbyist should try to keep only hardy, well-known species that are being bred in captivity. This may restrict your selections a bit, but it will also assure you of a better chance of success. Photo: G. Dingerkus.*

snakes are picked up immediately behind the head, i.e., in the neck region, without strong pressure being exerted. The use of forked sticks to pin the animals down on the ground often results in squeezing of the windpipe, which almost always ends in a slow, lingering death. Nor should one ever attempt to pin down a crawling snake with the foot because it is difficult to judge how much pressure is being applied and the animal might sustain severe internal injuries. A more considerate method of catching snakes, also applied in the case of lizards, is to use a noose of nylon fibers (in the past

Some snakes just should not be kept by beginners. The Wart Snake Acrochordus granulatus *is largely aquatic but seldom survives long in the aquaterrarium. Photo: R. D. Bartlett.*

these snares were made from horsehair and fishing silk), thin leather strips, or fine copper wire.

Move the noose in such a way that it remains in the cervical region when being tightened. If the thread is very thin and there is a danger that it might cause

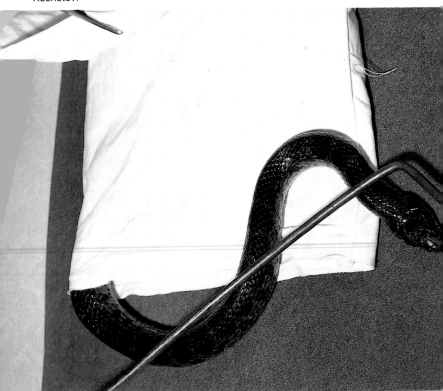

Using a snake stick to help remove a snake, Coluber hippocrepis, *from a collecting bag. Care must be used not to injure the snake's neck. Photo: S. Kochetov.*

Venomous snakes such as this Copperhead, Agkistrodon contortrix, *should be handled only with the help of a snake stick or similar tool. Photo: J. Dommers.*

cuts, several threads should be woven together and used as one. The collector is not, of course, being spared the task of having to disentangle and stow away the snake with the hand.

The most expedient packing material where snakes are concerned consists of canvas sacks, adapted to the snake's size and securely closed with string at the top. The animals travel inside these in normal, pressure-resistant cardboard boxes lined with a bit of moss. Canvas sacks have proved suitable mainly because the inmates frequently escape where other packing materials are being used.

On receipt of a snake consignment one should always check whether external parasites such as mites or ticks or remnants of the last sloughing have remained on the body.

Before putting the snake into its new home, it should be quarantined for a couple of weeks in a simple terrarium. If you were to put it directly into a planted tank, it might just disappear. Photo: B. Kahl.

Healthy snakes generally flick the tongue in a fairly lively manner and move in uninterrupted lines of waves. If these lines of locomotion are not continuous, the snakes concerned invariably suffer from spinal injuries. Further, when snakes are at rest, their bodies are always coiled, form drooping loops, or show modes of behavior that are characteristic of the species. What healthy snakes never do is remain stretched out in the terrarium. For the purpose of observation all new arrivals should be kept separately for a couple of weeks and be looked after with great care and attention before they are transferred to their permanent accommodation. This is all the more imperative if they are to live in association with other species of snakes.

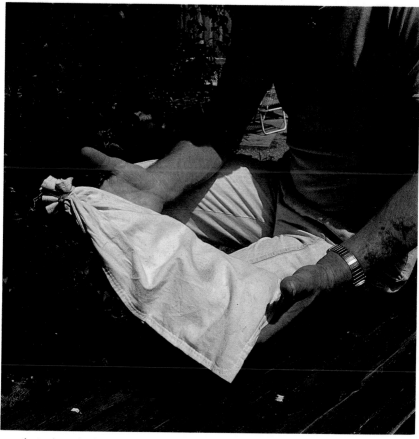

A sturdy snake bag is a must when collecting and also very handy for temporary storage while cleaning cages. Be sure all the seams are double-sewn and the tie string cannot work loose. Photo: S. and H. Miller.

The proper way to hold a moderately small harmless snake, in this case a garter snake, Thamnophis. Notice that the head is held firmly and the body is supported. Photo: S. and H. Miller.

Anatomy and Biology

Snakes (Ophidia) are vertebrates which, along with the lizard-like tuatara (Rhynchocephalia), lizards (Sauria), crocodiles and alligators (Crocodilia), and tortoises (Chelonia), form the class Reptilia.

A characteristic shared by all snakes is the absence of feet. Shoulder-girdle and sternum are, without exception, absent. Rudiments of the pelvic girdle, on the other hand, are found only in the "giant snakes" (Boidae) and a few other primitive groups; in some of these species they are actually still visible in

If you are a firm believer that your snake is completely tame, as is this captive-bred amelanic Corn Snake, Elaphe guttata, *you can trust it with a free head. Be sure to support the body, however. Photo: W. E. Burgess.*

the form of a movable anal claw in a pit-like depression on either side of the anal opening. These anal claws represent the vestiges of leg and foot bones that were originally present and have been lost in the course of evolution. The anal claws of the boas and pythons are used in mating; they function as auxiliary organs during copulation. The vestiges of a pelvic girdle are also found in blind snakes and slender blind snakes (typhlopids and leptotyphlopids).

In other groups of snakes the entire skeleton consists solely of the skull and a vertebral column of body length, with each vertebra— except the anterior vertebra and the caudal ones— bearing two ribs which are attached by movable joints and laterally pointing downward.

With the reptiles the actual transition to permanent terrestrial life among the animals that make up

the subphylum Vertebrata begins. This progression gave rise to a thickening of the horny epidermis and to a variety of differentiations of the external covering of the body, the integument. The entire body of the snake is covered in horny scales, with the areas between them

There are many legless lizards that closely resemble snakes in external appearance. This is an Eastern Glass Lizard, Ophisaurus ventralis. *As a general rule, legless lizards have eyelids and an external opening to the ear, as well as thick tongues with short tips. In most legless lizards the scalation does not resemble that of a snake if looked at closely, and there often are obvious remnants of legs visible externally. Photo: R. S. Simmons.*

being less strongly kerati-
nized. Hence the smooth
and elegant movements of
the snakes. On the head the
scales become small plates
and shields, the arrange-
ment and shape of which
are of the greatest signifi-

*Boas and pythons usually have "anal
claws," external remnants of a pair of
legs on each side of the anal opening.
Larger in males than females, they now
are used in courtship activity. Photo: S.
Kochetov.*

cance in the determination of the individual species. Conversely, on the ventral surfaces, the scales are strap-like and serve the purpose of locomotion.

The scale is nothing more than an outgrowth of the integument pointing backward. Its formation is due to an arching of the corium, the true skin, which in turn pushes the epidermis, the outermost skin, before it. The marked keratinization of the

This cleared and stained water snake, Nerodia sipedon, *shows the great number of vertebrae and ribs found in the average snake. The loosely attached jaws are also obvious. Photo: G. Dingerkus.*

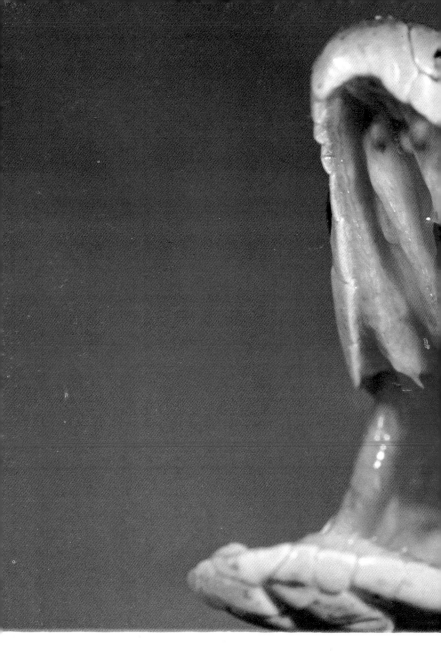

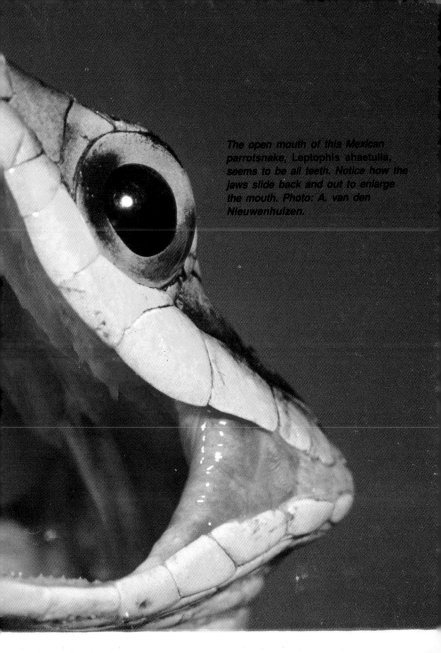

The open mouth of this Mexican parrotsnake, *Leptophis ahaetulla*, seems to be all teeth. Notice how the jaws slide back and out to enlarge the mouth. Photo: A. van den Nieuwenhuizen.

external skin prevents a constant growth of the snakes, which is why a periodic renewal (ecdysis) is necessary, known to the lay person as shedding or sloughing. A dirty and rough appearance of the snake's skin and disinterest in food are the first external signs that sloughing is imminent. Further, a milky-white turbidity of the fluid under the "spectacles" (a single transparent scale representing the fused eyelids) sets in, as well as the growth of special hair-like processes which effect the mechanical lifting-off of the old skin that is to be cast from the newly formed skin lying beneath it. Due to the blood vessels of the anterior end becoming engorged with blood, the head swells up immediately prior to sloughing so that as the swelling recedes, the detachment of the old skin is initiated, starting along the edges of the jaws. As a rule the skin is cast in its entirety and in one piece.

As opposed to the amphibians, reptiles possess hardly any glands in the skin; in snakes they are virtually absent. Where they do exist their function is connected with reproduction. Examples are the thigh glands of lizards and the musk gland on the lower jaw of crocodiles.

What characterizes the skull of a snake is the great flexibility of the individual bones—their ability to move away from each other. The bones are connected to each other by elastic ligaments. The joint between the upper and lower jaws is situated well back to enable the snakes to open their jaws and prise them apart as widely as possible. Only a small part of the bones of the skull encase the brain so that the membrane bones of the skull, too, are able to move sideways and backward at any time. The two halves of the lower jaw are connected anteriorly by

When a snake opens its mouth, the many rows of teeth in the upper jaws become obvious. This parrotsnake, Leptophis mexicanus, is notorious for its vicious bites. Photo: K. T. Nemuras.

Some snakes can swallow enormous prey. This Plain Eggeater, Dasypeltis inornata, *is preparing to swallow a chicken egg. Photos: A. van den Nieuwenhuizen.*

As the Eggeater succeeds in swallowing the egg, notice the tremendous flexibility of the bones of the head and the skin behind the head. Photos: A. van den Nieuwenhuizen.

The forward position of the fang of this Copperhead, Agkistrodon contortrix, *is obvious in this photo. Notice that the fang is folded back when not in use and erected when the mouth opens. Photo: J. Gee.*

elastic ligaments; this enables them to move independently of one another.

All these peculiarities in the structure of the snake's skull became necessary in adaptation to the snake's feeding mechanism. Although most groups of snakes possess fully formed teeth and tooth-like processes, these are merely sitting on top of the jaw bone and are replaced when they are worn away. This phenomenon is described as polyphyodonty. The teeth are never used for breaking down the food. The prey, whether killed or still alive, is always swallowed whole. For this reason the skull must be able to withstand an incredible amount of stress, considering that snakes of medium size manage to engulf a bird or a mouse without difficulty.

The poison teeth are special structures used in procuring food and as a means of defense. All sorts of transitions are found, from the simple fang of a Grass Snake (*Natrix natrix*) to the "classic" structure of the poison tooth such as that of the Adder (*Vipera berus*).

The basic conditions for the venomous bite are already present in the

Although it is a rear-fang, the Boomslang, Dispholidus typus, *is especially dangerous because the fangs are rather long and are located almost under the eye, far enough forward to allow them to be used in bites of larger objects such as legs and arms. Photo: J. Visser.*

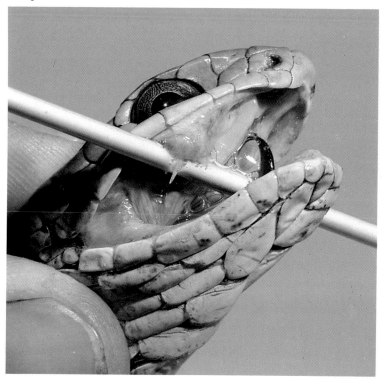

aglyphs, the smooth-toothed snakes, in the form of non-functional or barely functional venom-secreting glandular segments such as those of the Grass Snake step further. Here the venom is assisted in reaching the site of the wound by an open groove on the back of the tooth. The venom is not injected,

Some of the long-snouted arboreal vine snakes such as this Ahaetulla nasuta *have horizontal pupils with a distinctive keyhole or figure-eight shape. This helps the snake "aim" down a groove on the elongated snout. Photo: C. Banks.*

(*Natrix natrix*). In these cases, however, a poison duct in or on the tooth is always absent.

The opisthoglyphs or rear-fanged snakes go one

Facing page: *This green tree viper,* Trimeresurus stejnegeri, *is taking a white mouse several times the bulk of its head. Photo: A. van den Nieuwenhuizen.*

however, until the prey has already been partially swallowed, since the teeth are not situated anteriorly but near the pharynx. This is an additional measure for the quick killing of prey which, due to the emission of digestive secretions, probably also initiates an early commencement of digestion.

The poison fangs of true venomous snakes are situated anteriorly in the upper jaw. Depending on the structure, we differentiate between two types: firstly, the groove-toothed proteroglyphs and, secondly, the solenoglyphs with fistular teeth. In the former, the groove is almost enclosed whereas in the solenoglyphs a proper canal

Most snakes take their prey head-first; because the hairs, feathers, or scales tend to point backward, prey ingested tail-first would be hard to swallow. Photo: A. van den Nieuwenhuizen.

runs through the tooth.

Gustatory organs in the form of taste buds are frequently present inside the oral cavity of snakes. They are also found on the tongue, on the roof on the mouth and, in venomous snakes, in the proximity of the poison fangs.

The most important sensory perception in the life of a snake is carried out by the sense of smell. A special organ known as Jacobson's organ, which consists of two pits lined with a sensory epithelial tissue, has the function of detecting prey and enemies as well as that of olfactory orientation in the snake's habitat. Due to the constant flickering of the tongue, the minute particles of scent are picked up and transported to the pits of Jacobson's organ since the latter's ducts are connected to the oral cavity.

The optic sense, too, is well-developed in snakes, although most forms are

A Tentacled Snake, Erpeton tentaculatum, *prepares to catch and swallow a Goldfish. Photos: A. van den Nieuwenhuizen.*

stimulated into perception only by movements and changes. This also explains why food animals are not identified as such until they jump about or crawl.

The hearing capacity is comparatively undeveloped in reptiles. In snakes it is said to be completely absent. The tympanic cavity is, without exception, absent in all snakes.

As is to be expected, considering the elongated body, the internal organs also became elongated to a greater or lesser extent. Of the digestive tract only the gullet, capable of enormous dilation in snakes, and the stomach shall be mentioned here.

The liver is long, elongated and without lobes. A gall bladder is present,

Although the Tentacled Snake probably is one of the most distinctive of snakes because of the obvious scaly projections or tentacles, no one is certain exactly what these projections do. It is assumed that they somehow help the snake locate prey (such as the barb shown above), but the method is unknown. Photos: A. van den Nieuwenhuizen.

too.

The pancreas is situated between the stomach and the proximal segment of the small intestine. A urinary bladder is absent in snakes. The ureters dischage their contents straight into the cloaca, from which feces and urine are then excreted together.

In skinks and many anguids (lizards of a snake-like structure) there is a reduction of the left lung. In snakes this is even more pronounced. The right lung is very elongated and its

posterior segment has been transformed into a smooth-walled sac for storing air reserves. It does not contain any respiratory pulmonary epithelium for absorbing oxygen. The air reservoir maintains the supply of respiratory oxygen during the act of prey-engulfment.

In snakes and in many other reptiles, the complete separation of the arterial and venous circulation of the blood has evolved further. In the ventricle (chamber of the heart) there is a septum which does not entirely separate the two chambers, however.

The kidneys of snakes are long and narrow, richly lobed. They lie one behind the other.

The testes and ovaries are also staggered. The latter appear lobed. The penises of the males are present in

The course of prey down the digestive tract of a snake can be followed by noting how distended are the scales. As the prey is digested, the skin assumes a more normal appearance. Photos: A. van den Nieuwenhuizen.

pairs. Only one of them (the hemipenis) is inserted into the female cloaca, however. The seminal fluid enters the female sexual partner via a groove, not a canal. After copulation the whole copulatory apparatus, extroverted like the finger of a glove, is pulled back into its original position behind the cloaca by means of a retractor muscle situated in the tail.

The vast majority of snakes are oviparous. The eggs—usually oval, with a parchment-like shell—are deposited in pits of varying depths at selected localities. Viviparous forms also exist, however. One example is the Adder (*Vipera berus*), which gives birth to numerous young snakes already of considerable size.

The eggs are laid two months or more after fertilization. That, then, is how much time elapses from successful insemination to the maturation of the egg. The gestation period generally lies between 4 and 12 weeks, although here again plenty of exceptions to the rule could be cited. During this period the eggs increase significantly in

Most snakes are oviparous, laying eggs that hatch outside the mother's body. These little Horned Vipers, Cerastes cerastes, *are just emerging from the eggs. Photo: K. H. Switak.*

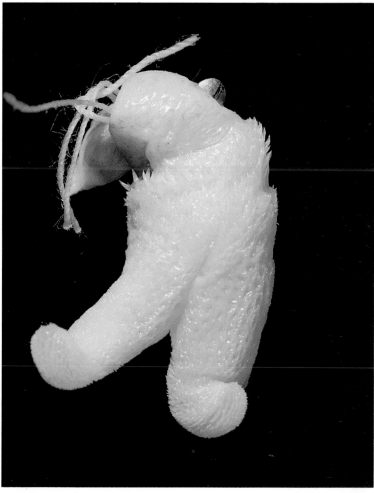

The copulatory organ of a male snake is a split or paired structure known as the hemipenes. Hemipenes often contain features useful in classification. These are the preserved hemipenes of a cobra, Naja nivea. *Photo: J. Visser.*

both diameters.

Just before hatching, the eggs grow wrinkled and several cuts, caused by the egg-tooth of the hatching snake, become visible. Eventually the young animal leaves the egg through one of the openings that have been cut into the shell.

Every animal owner will endeavor to get the animals in his or her care to breed in captivity. In a sense, a successful propagation confirms that the animals are being properly kept and cared for. As compared with other groups of reptiles, snakes are relatively easy to breed, all the more so since there are livebearing species as well, as already mentioned.

Furthermore, if the keeper makes at least some effort to meet the snakes' requirements, these animals go on for a long time in captivity. Often they attain an age which in their natural environment it would hardly be possible for

them to reach. A Leopard Snake (*Elaphe situla*), for example, lived to the age of 25 years. Various pythons and boas have lived beyond the age of 15 years.

Anyone who keeps snakes will be aware that it is sometimes unavoidable to handle objects inside the container, to remove leftovers, feces, or waste—in short, to carry out the various tasks necessary to ensure the proper maintenance of the terrarium. All hurried movements should be avoided. The keeper must proceed gently and with caution, particularly where he knows the inmates to be aggressive, liable to bite, or otherwise dangerous. In order to play it absolutely safe and be protected against the bites of non-venomous snakes, too (which are, after all, unpleasantly painful), suitable boxes should be supplied for the snakes to retreat into. These should be

Birth in a Copperhead, Agkistrodon contortrix. *Notice that the hatchling is surrounded by a membranous bag that actually is one of the egg membranes. Livebearing snakes often are though of as merely retaining the eggs inside the body through incubation and never completing a shell on the egg. Photo: R. T. Zappalorti.*

put inside the terrarium a few hours before the work is intended to be carried out and they should be closed from the outside once the snakes have gone in. This also ensures that the snakes are not being troubled in any way and avoids having to catch the animals with the hands.

If in spite of all caution and conscientiousness a keeper of poisonous snakes still has the misfortune to be bitten by a snake, then a firm tourniquet must be applied to the injured hand or arm at once (above, and not too close to, the bite wound) and a doctor be called immediately. Nobody, not even an experienced snake keeper, should make the mistake of trying to assess the bite and its consequences himself, let alone to make light of it. It is vital to do everything possible to counteract the toxic effect of the bite.

If it has been decided to keep some species of venomous snake or other, it is absolutely essential to get hold of a specific or polyvalent serum at the same time and never forget to replace the latter before the date stated on the packet. Serums which are old and have been stored for too long are totally useless since they no longer have any effect after the stated period.

The toxic effect of a snake bite varies a lot, depending on what species the snake belongs to. Often even related species differ in this

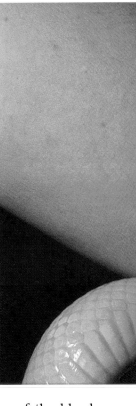

respect. Effusion of blood, inflammations, and necroses are the first local effects of venomous bites. The bite of a viper results in the dissolution of the red blood cells. Most snake poisons cause damage to the circulation of the blood and cardiac weakness. Circulatory disturbances of the capillaries and extensive effusions of blood occur conjointly with highly dangerous attacks of cardiac weakness.

Even a tame snake will bite if it feels cornered or is surprised by a sudden movement. This captive-bred albino California Kingsnake, Lampropeltis getulus californiae, *is doing its best to inflict damage, but its teeth are too small. Photo: J. Wines.*

The poisons of cobras and a few vipers cause a respiratory paralysis, due to suppressing the nervous control of the respiratory musculature, which results in death if not properly treated. The venom of the South American Rattlesnake, *Crotalus durissus terrificus*, if not administered in the lethal dose by the bite, leads to blindness.

In addition, true nerve toxins as well as metabolic and glandular poisons are known. The latter can, for example, cause a serious increase in the blood-sugar level due to upsetting the secretory activity of the pancreas.

When this Indian Cobra, Naja naja, comes out of the snake charmer's basket, it means business. The bite of a cobra is a classic example of neurotoxic venom. Photo: R. T. Zappalorti.

Foods and Feeding

The only food that is suitable for snakes—all snakes—under normal circumstances is live food animals. As a rule these consist of vertebrates, rarely arthropods, worms and slugs. Many small burrowing snakes will accept earthworms, centipedes, and ants. No snakes will accept vegetarian food.

Fish are greatly liked particularly by the water snakes. The catching of native fish for the purpose of feeding terrarium animals

*Because snakes cannot chew their food (they have only pointed teeth and their jaws are too delicate anyway), they must swallow all prey whole. Although some will take relatively gigantic food items (such as the Common Eggeater, Dasypeltis scabra, on the facing page), most prefer smaller items such as the Fathead Minnow below. Photos: **Facing page:** A. van den Nieuwenhuizen; **Below:** A. Norman.*

often meets with difficulties from the authorities. The simplest way is for the snake keeper to purchase feeder fishes from a pet shop or live bait store. Fish farms are another source of supply. They often sell young fish at comparatively low prices. However, to avoid seasonal problems it is a good idea to breed the fish oneself. Fish which are particularly suitable for this are the livebearers that originate from Central and South America—for instance the Guppy (*Poecilia reticulata*) or the Swordtail (*Xiphophorus helleri*) in all its different varieties. The animals spawn frequently and produce a considerable number of easily raised fry on each occasion. Furthermore, they are relatively undemanding as regards keeping, feeding, and care. All-glass tanks of the dimensions 30 x 30 x 25

Xenopus laevis is one of the few frogs that can be cultured readily or purchased on a regular basis at local pet shops. Photo: K. Lucas.

Although most snakes prefer living prey, many can be trained to accept frozen and thoroughly thawed foods. Corn Snakes, Elaphe guttata, *such as this captive-bred specimen, will accept frozen foods from birth. Photo: K. H. Switak.*

Some hobbyists never lose their fascination with seeing a snake swallow very large prey. Shown is the Common Eggeater, Dasypeltis scabra. *Photos: A. van den Nieuwenhuizen.*

cm, say, are adequate as breeding containers. Where the diet consists of marine fishes it must be supplemented with vitamins (in drop form) to avoid dangerous deficiency diseases.

A great proportion of snakes, however, prefer amphibians and other reptiles, including members of their own species in some cases. There is no way one can breed these animals oneself since the development from the egg to the adult extends over a prolonged period during which the brood needs a great deal of care and attention if it is to thrive and remain healthy. During the first few days of their terrestrial life following the completion of their development, ranid frogs can be readily caught in large quantities and can then be kept and tended

Mice only a day or two old, before they become covered with hair, are called pinkies or pink mice by hobbyists. They are acceptable by many small and medium snakes. Photo: W. B. Allen, Jr.

An Eastern Kingsnake, Lampropeltis getulus getulus, *constricting its prey, a Black Racer. In captivity, constricting snakes fed frozen food seldom waste energy constricting dead prey. Photo: W. B. Allen, Jr.*

until required as food. Newts can be found on the edges of ponds and under big stones. Tree frogs are eaten with relish, notably by the South American tree snakes. Sparrows, both adults and nestlings, are excellently suited as food for snakes.

Remember, however, that many areas have laws prohibiting or regulating the taking of amphibians and all oher animals in quantity. Be sure to check your local laws before collecting any vertebrates as potential pets or live foods.

Although, generally speaking, motionless food is rejected by snakes, there are some specialists as well, for instance the African Egg-eating Snake (*Dasypeltis scabra*), which feeds on the eggs of birds and reptiles. Certain European snakes occasionally eat eggs, the Four-lined snake (*Elaphe quatuorlineata*) being a case in point.

Of the small mammals, white mice, rats, Syrian golden hamsters, and guinea pigs have proved well suited. The culture of these rodents is very productive and easy. For larger varieties such as the giant snakes (boids and pythons) tame young hares are more suitable.

The snakes kill their prey in various ways. The giant snakes dispatch the food animals by constriction and strangulation. The Ringed Snake (*Natrix natrix*) grabs the prey and swallows it alive, whereby the teeth, curved backwards like barbs, prevent escape. Yet others kill or paralyze their victims with a poisonous bite prior to devouring them. No snake tears the prey to pieces; the food animal is always gulped down whole.

Generally speaking, snakes should be fed two to three times a week. However, where the giant snakes are concerned it is sufficient to supply food once a week or at even longer intervals.

Often the animals refuse food for weeks on end. When this happens there is no reason to fear they have become victims of some insidious disease. First, try to get them to eat again by offering as varied a diet as possible. If all efforts fail, however, as is often the case with animals that have only recently arrived or been freshly caught, then there is no alternative but to force-feed them. This is done by picking the snake up and pushing the food down its gullet. (Usually this presents no problem since the excitement causes the snake to open its jaws.) Multi-vitamin preparations can be administered at the same

Many hobbyists find it necessary to force-feed a snake that is not eating on its own. Force-feeding is a technique best learned by watching someone else do it rather than reading about it. It can also be dangerous to both the snake and, if the snake is a vicious or semivenomous species such as this Mangrove Snake, Boiga dendrophila, *to the keeper. Photo: S. Kochetov.*

time, and it is advisable to treat the food with these beforehand. Suitable foods that can be used for force-feeding are pieces of meat, strips of liver, etc., and yolk of egg. To speed up the act of swallowing, gentle tugging at the solid food is recommended to simulate the wriggling movements of live prey. It must be pointed out, however, that force-feeding should be undertaken only in hopeless cases since it all too easily results in injuries to the pharyngeal mucous membranes if carried out inexpertly. Furthermore, snakes are able to survive without food for considerable periods of time without there being any cause for concern on the keeper's part.

Ticks are basically giant, armored mites. There are several species of small (barely visible to the naked eye) ticks found only on snakes, but most of the ticks the hobbyist is likely to encounter are fairly normal species similar to cat and dog ticks in shape and even size. When noticed, especially on recent imports, they should be removed before they can do further harm. Because snakes squirm, only blunt instruments or forceps should be used for removal, never a regular knifeblade. Photo: W. B. Allen, Jr. of Python sebae.

Diseases of Snakes

Even in terraria that have been set up to a high standard and where care and maintenance are all they should be, there can be incidents of illness and contagious diseases from time to time. Usually, the changed behavior of his snakes will alert the good observer to the early stages of a disease and he will isolate the affected specimens by transferring them to individual cages. Once the sick animal has been moved into a quarantine cage it can be given whatever specific treatment may be necessary without being able to harm any of the other snakes.

If a snake listlessly lies about in the terrarium and the characteristic flicking of the tongue has ceased, these are early warning signs of ill health. Any animal which shows this suspect behavior should be given a thorough examination so that the causes of its abnormal behavior can be established as quickly as possible.

Close-ups of ticks removed from a Boa Constrictor. The larger specimen probably is a female, the smaller one a male. Photo: Dr. Fredric L. Frye, from his book Reptile Care.

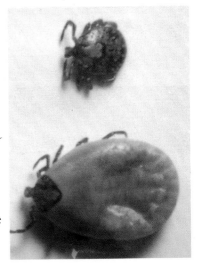

Snakes are often infested with ticks and mites of various types. Ticks often occur in newly imported specimens and should be pulled out when the snake is first examined before quarantine. Snake ticks usually are small and just a nuisance, but they do take quite a bit of blood and may spread other parasites.

With the aid of specially adapted mouthparts, mites take blood and lymph from the host's body. Most of the ectoparasitic mites live on, beneath, or between the scales. Some forms, however, colonize the edges of the eyes which in cases of more severe infestation can lead to blindness. Yet others live as internal parasites inside the parenchyma of the lungs on which they feed.

The primary damage suffered by the host animals obviously is the blood loss. Frequently, however, there are secondary infections as well to which the body of the host, already weakened, has become particularly susceptible.

The preparations and chemicals to be used in the control of ectoparasites must be chosen with extreme caution. There are numerous contact insectides which can cause severe symptoms of poisoning if administered in the most minute quantities, and one cannot issue too strong a warning in this respect. After making convulsive and reeling movements, the animals poisoned in this way often die within the shortest possible time.

In the control of mites, good results have been achieved with camphor chloride. The white, slightly volatile powder is scattered in a dry all-glass container, the affected snake is put in, and the treatment container is rendered airtight. After about 80 minutes all the mites will be destroyed. Here, too, however, the snake's behavior must be

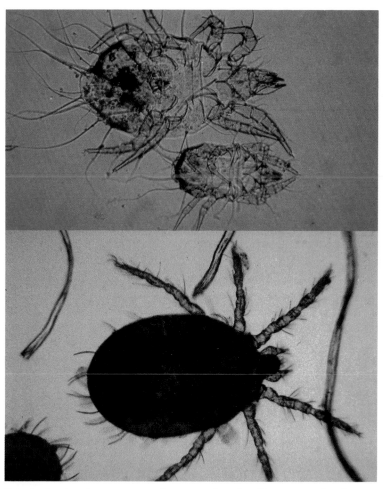

Not all mites found on or near snakes are snake mites. These are grain mites, probably brought in with food or the substrate. Notice that the mite in the bottom photo has only three pairs of legs—it is a nymphal stage. Photos: Dr. Fredric L. Frye, from his book Reptile Care.

carefully monitored throughout. If signs of poisoning occur the animal must be transferred to a well-ventilated, warmed container where it will normally make a quick recovery. Where only a few areas of the body are infested with mites these can be treated with cooking oil (applied with a brush) which should kill the mites. The parasites have also been effectively controlled with a good cod liver oil ointment which is rubbed into the whole body of the snake. The ointment has the added advantage of speeding up the healing of wounds that have been caused by the mites.

Sloughing, which, depending on the species, occurs regularly at intervals of several weeks to several months, is of the greatest

All snakes shed their skins, though the interval between sheds may vary tremendously depending on age, temperature, and feeding habits. Photo: J. Dommers.

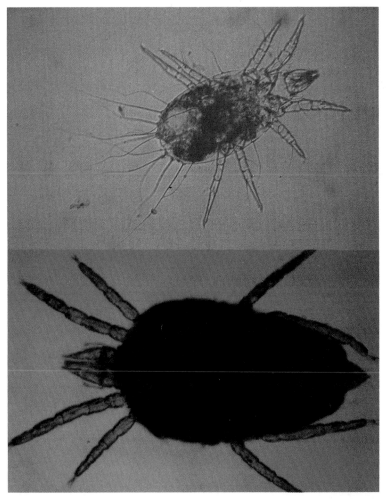

Mites usually are almost microscopic and have four pairs of legs in the adults. Identification of mites is complex and beyond the reach of amateurs. Photos: Dr. Fredric L. Frye, from his book Reptile Care.

The black spots on this rat snake are melanosarcomas, a type of skin cancer. Photo: E. Elkan.

significance as an indicator of well-being. In normal cases the old skin detaches itself in one piece like a tube. At this time the eyes grow clouded, the animals lose their appetite, and eventually the old skin which is to be cast bursts open along the labial edges and the snake slips out of its garment, often crawling about among shrubs and on objects with rough surfaces to aid the sloughing process purely mechanically.

Where the snake-keeper observes that the molt is not running its normal course he should provide bathing facilities or resolve the problem by immersing the snake in tepid water for two to three hours. The forcible removal of any pieces of skin that are still adhering must

Blue eyes are a good indication that a snake is about to shed. Fluid has begun to accumulate between the old and new skins (the covering of the eye is a modified piece of transparent skin) and shedding should occur within one to three days. Photo: J. Dommers.

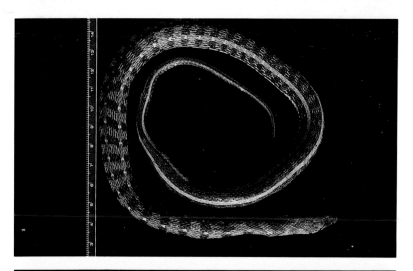

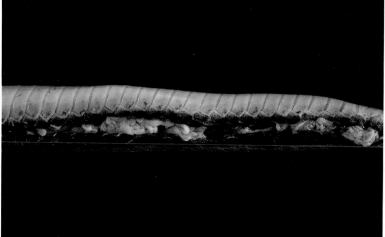

Cestodes (tapeworms) are common parasites in snakes, especially snakes that eat fishes on a regular basis. Not only can mature tapes be found in the gut, but larval stages often end up trapped (encysted) under the skin, resulting in large lumps as in the water snake shown above. Photos: Dr. Fredric L. Frye, from his book Reptile Care.

be avoided. A method which has proved successful in such cases is to rub cod liver oil ointment into the skin. Afterward these remnants are cast without difficulty.

Parasitic worms have been found in virtually all groups of vertebrates. It is not surprising, therefore, that we also know of a great many worms which parasitize on snakes. Above all cestodes (tapeworms), trematodes (flukes, unsegmented flatworms with adhesive suckers), and nematodes (roundworms or threadworms) occur most frequently. It would be far beyond the scope of this book to provide an even remotely exhaustive report on the material known to date. In an infestation with

Intestinal enlargement ("bloating") in a rat snake caused by a type of protozoan, the coccidian Cryptosporidium. *Photo: Dr. Fredric L. Frye, from his book* Reptile Care.

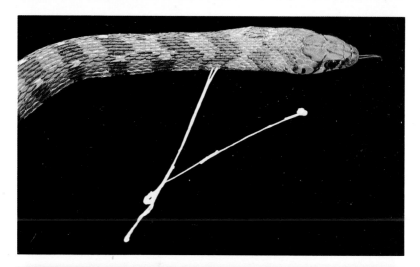

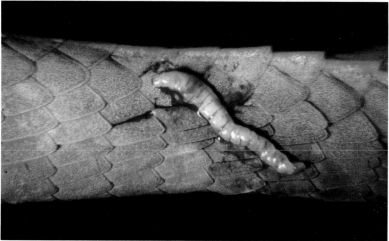

Top: *Plerocercoids (tapeworm larvae) being removed from under the skin of a water snake.* **Bottom:** *A pentastomid (tongueworm) freshly removed from under the skin of a vine snake. Photos: Dr. Fredric L. Frye, from his book* Reptile Care.

Although this kingsnake, Lampropeltis alterna, *looks like it has just had a heavy meal, it actually is suffering from a coccidian infection. Photo: Dr. Fredric L. Frye, from his book* Reptile Care.

parasitic worms it is not only the intestinal tract that is colonized but also the musculature, the subcutaneous tissue, and nearly all the internal organs. On the one hand, the harm which is done by worms that live in the gut lies in the extraction of valuable nutrients and where other worms are involved it consists of the active destruction of parts of organs. In all cases, however, the greatest damage is due to the excretion of metabolic waste products and their toxic effects inside the host's body.

Good results in the control of the worms can be achieved with anthelminthics commonly used for small children. These must be administered together with laxatives,

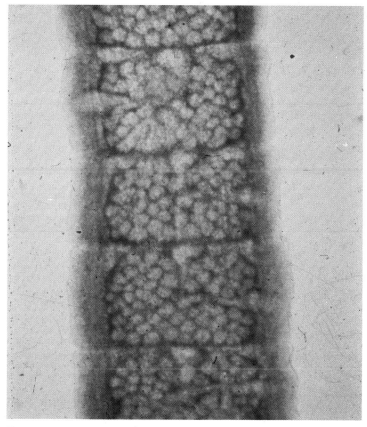

The mature reproductive segments of a tapeworm. These egg-filled segments are called proglottids. Photo: E. Elkan.

Severe mouth rot (stomatitis) in a Boa Constrictor. This particular snake probably is beyond recovery. Mouth rot is the most dreaded disease likely to strike pet snakes. Photo: W. B. Allen, Jr.

ensuring that the gut is emptied quickly.

The disease known as pox is a collective name applied to several conditions that run a similar course. The recommended treatment consists of the administration of antibiotics such as penicillin, terramycin, and aureomycin. The drugs are given either by injection or orally. It is important that the dosage is not too low. Rather, it should be exceeded slightly to make sure the causal agents do not become resistant. For a snake measuring about 40 cm in length a dose of 1000 I.U. (International Units) would be appropriate. Terramycin and aureomycin hardly ever cause harmful side effects. In the case of penicillin, on the other hand, these can be observed from time to time. The healing of the wounds can be speeded up considerably by additional local treatment of the pox with silver nitrate and a combination of aureomycin and sulphonamide.

The most dreaded snake disease is known as "mouth rot." It is likely to be a complex of several diseases which have a causative connection with each other. The animals stop flicking the tongue, the epithelium inside the oral cavity grows pale, small white speckles and little yellowish lumps lie scattered on the upper lining of the oral cavity and pharynx. As the disease progresses these abnormalities extend to the air passages, the gums start to break down in patches, and the teeth drop out. The causal agent was found to be *Aeromonas fluorescens liquefaciens*. Provided the disease is detected in its early stages, it can be reversed by means of a 3% solution of hydrogen peroxide applied to the oral cavity and pharynx with a brush. Further effective treatment of this illness

This stomatitis infection seems to be restricted to the base of the fangs of this puff adder. With immediate attention and persistent treatment by the hobbyist, the snake is likely to recover. Photo: W. B. Allen, Jr.

consists of prolonged baths in and injections of vitamin C (ascorbic acid). Ideally this should be followed by rinsing with quinoline (1 tablet of quinoline per tumbler of water) several times a day. In the last few years the antiseptic "Listerine" has turned out to be very effective in the control of "mouth rot." "Mouth rot" type diseases described in more recent reports have also been attributed to avitaminoses.

No less dangerous are the disorders of the digestive tract. In the Boidae, sudden deaths can usually be traced back to gangrenous inflammation of the intestinal lumen. The disease runs a rapid course; affected animals often die after a few days. A still more common cause of dangerous intestinal disease is constipation. Of great benefit in these cases is treatment with warm baths and the administration of castor oil via the food.

Extraordinarily vulnerable are the respiratory organs of snakes. Even minor injuries in the region of the throat and windpipe caused by

A Reticulated Python, Python reticulatus, *with metal sutures holding together a severe laceration caused by a fight with a cage mate. Photo: W. B. Allen, Jr.*

catching the animals with forked sticks can result in death within a few days.

Pneumonia, which occurs in the spring from time to time, has a fatal outcome in most cases. The animals raise the anterior end of the body perpendicularly, the lung is over-inflated, the mouth wide open. If the disease is recognized at a very early stage, it can be cured with eucalyptus oil, partly because snakes often exhibit such symptoms without suffering from true pneumonia. Tuberculosis infections have also been diagnosed in snakes occasionally.

Deficiency diseases and avitaminoses are more easily prevented than cured. If the diet is sufficiently varied, these conditions rarely occur in snakes. What is important above all is to make sure the food animals are properly nourished. Where necessary, weekly supplements of multi-vitamin preparations should be given. These can readily be injected into the dorsal lymph sac of frogs before the latter are fed to the snakes. Over and above that, it is advisable during the cold season to replace the natural light conditions with an ultraviolet lamp for about 10 to 15 minutes each day.

Surgical intervention, such as the removal of tumors, applying a clamp to larger flesh wounds, etc., is best left to the veterinary specialist, who will administer a urethane anesthetic.

Fractures, notably injuries to the vertebral column which are instantly recognizable during locomotion by the interruption of the continuous sinusoidal line, are immobilized by applying firm wooden splints or cardboard sleeves and left to heal.

Species

Inasfar as the scope of this book permits, this section will provide the most important facts about the origin, appearance, and dietary requirements of the species of snakes that are suitable for being kept in captivity.

Many species, including some which are fairly well-known, cannot receive mention here since they are unsuitable for keeping in the terrarium. For this reason the Wart Snakes

Although juvenile Wart Snakes such as this Acrochordus javanicus *are sold, they are unsuitable as pets and should not be purchased by amateurs. Photo: K. T. Nemuras.*

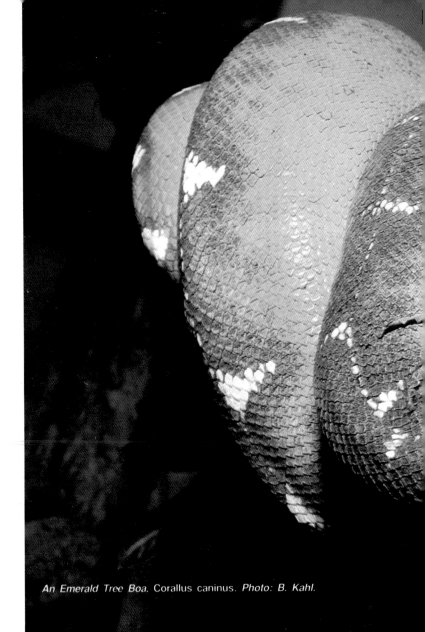
An Emerald Tree Boa. Corallus caninus. *Photo: B. Kahl.*

(Acrochordidae) and Sea Snakes (Hydrophiidae), for instance, have been omitted. The individual descriptions of the species are intended to encourage the study of the special literature.

GIANT SNAKES
Boidae

It should not really be necessary to point out that terraria for giant snakes must be large, spacious containers with strong glass. Special furnishings are not required. On the contrary, the interior should be kept as simple as possible so that the containers can readily be cleaned at any time and a high standard of cleanliness can be maintained. The bottom should be covered with fine gravel, sand, or a mixture of peat and sand. A large water container, securely built in, is essential. The giant snakes often lie inside these for days and their feces are deposited there as well. The water container also serves as a drinking vessel, however; most giant snakes take in water by means of chewing/scooping movements with the lower jaw. It is vital, therefore, that the water container be kept clean. Baths are extremely important since they aid the regular sloughing process. As regards the water temperature, the snakes are not over-sensitive. Strong climbing branches—very popular with the animals— should never be absent, especially when true climbers such as the Emerald Tree Boa (*Corallus caninus*) are being kept. During the day the room temperature inside the terrarium for giant snakes should be within the range of about 26 to 29°C. At night it can safely be allowed to drop to 20 to 22°C.

Giant snakes are mostly active at dusk. For this reason, their food animals should always be put into the terrarium toward the

The Boa Constrictor, Boa constrictor, still is moderately common in the pet market but now is quite expensive. Juveniles often die of respiratory diseases and parasites. Photo: B. Kahl.

Snakes are identified by details of scalation of the head, among other features. Because so many species have similar patterns and scale counts, it often is impossible to identify photographs of specimens from unknown localities. Photo: S. Kochetov.

evening. The keeper needs to make sure that the supply of food does not exceed the demand. Leftover food animals—rats and mice, for example—may not only pester the snake but can actually nibble at the resting snake's body. Where two snakes are being kept in one container it is possible that both of them would seize the same prey and the bigger snake gulp down the smaller one with the food animal if the keeper does not step in quickly and drive one of them away with tobacco smoke or the vapors of liquid ammonia.

The prey is grasped by means of a quick forward thrust and is instantly constricted, resulting in asphyxiation of the prey animal. The snake does not uncoil until the prey is dead. Some giant snakes in captivity can be acclimatized to accepting food-animals that have already been killed. Just as enormous as the quantities of food that can be consumed by a hungry giant snake in one week is the capacity to fast and refuse all food. When it comes to selecting their prey, different animals of the same species often show considerable individual variations, and food that was accepted for months on end may suddenly, inexplicably, be refused. Digestion proceeds rapidly.

A hatching Indian Python, Python molurus. *The full arrowhead marking identifies this snake as the eastern subspecies,* P. m. bivittatus. *Photo: B. Kahl.*

As snakes are bred in captivity more commonly, variations in pattern are found and pleasing variations will become established in the hobby. This variant Royal Python, Python regius, *has a broad golden vertebral stripe. Photo: R. D. Bartlett.*

Indigestible parts such as claws, horns, teeth, and feathers as well as plants from the gut of digested animals are regurgitated.

The giant snakes are very ancient animals. Vestiges of a pelvic girdle and the vestigial hindlimbs—externally slightly more evident in male than in female animals because of the former's more conspicuous claws on the legs—are present in both boas and pythons, as are paired lungs. Apart from minor differences in the skeletal structure of the head, the two groups differ in the way they reproduce. Boas give birth to living young whereas pythons lay eggs. The facial pits between the scales bordering the upper lip sometimes are clearly visible in the giant snakes. These are organs for the perception of fluctuations in temperature, closely related in their function to the "pit" of the crotalids (pit vipers). One group of boids, namely the sand boas of the genus *Eryx*, do not, strictly speaking, deserve the name "giant snakes." They barely attain a length of more than 1 m.

The best-known of all boids, always available on the market and widely kept, is the Boa Constrictor (*Boa constrictor*). It originates in tropical America and its range extends from the coasts of Mexico to Paraguay and northern Argentina. The color of these animals is magnificent and they show large spots distributed over the whole of the back. Particularly popular are young animals. When they are born they measure 35 to 45 cm in length. Within six months they grow to 70 to 80 cm long, and animals of one year of age reach a length of up to 125 cm.

The Imperial Boa (*Boa constrictor imperator*) inhabits the Pacific coast of much of Central and South America. This snake sometimes exceeds 3.6 m in length. The Argentine Boa (*Boa constrictor occidentalis*) is native to the arid steppes of South America, notably Argentina, as its name suggests. Its favorite food consists of pigeons and chickens.

The most popular Boa Constrictors, Boa constrictor, *are the red-tailed variants with distinctly red dorsal saddles posteriorly. This is the Surinam Red-Tail. Photo: R. D. Bartlett.*

The range of the largest of the giant snakes, the Anaconda (*Eunectes murinus*), extends over much of northern South back. Conspicuous is the light brown to brownish red band on both sides of the head which goes from the eye to the corner of the

America, especially the Orinoco and Amazon basins.

The basic color is olive-gray to brownish green, and two rows of big, round, dark brown spots run along the

A baby Anaconda, Eunectes murinus. *Their size, aggressiveness, and need for large water containers make Anacondas poor choices as pets. Photo: G. Dingerkus.*

The head pattern of a Boa Constrictor is very distinctive. No other boa has the combination of a narrow line over the top of the head plus the broad, dark oblique line back from the eye. The dorsal pattern varies with subspecies, locality, and individual but remains recognizable. Photo: P. J. Stafford.

The Madagascar Boa, Acrantophis madagascariensis, is not common in the hobby. Photo: K. H. Switak.

mouth. There have been many fantastic reports about the Anaconda's length, both verbally and in writing. Lengths of 7 to 8 m do occur. The biggest Anaconda described by credible sources is said to have measured 9.40 m. They are water-loving snakes. Often they lie in the water basin for days on end. For this reason they accept not only small mammals but also reptiles and fish. In their natural habitat they frequently devour caimans with great relish. A smaller member of the same genus is the Paraguay or Yellow Anaconda (*Eunectes notaeus*).

A very beautiful boid with a blue and green metallic sheen is *Acrantophis madagascariensis*. This species, at one time classified as belonging to the genus *Boa*, is very delicate and very susceptible to "mouth rot."

Liable to bite and rather aggressive is *Sanzinia madagascariensis*, a true tree dweller like its South American relative, the Emerald Tree Boa (*Corallus caninus*), which grows to over 2 m in length. Immature Emeralds show a rust brown coloration which changes into a leaf green after several molts. On the back there is a white line, sometimes interrupted, from which white crossbands extend at regular intervals. The scales on the upper lip and the underside are bright yellow. The terrarium of the Emerald Tree Boa must be richly planted and offer adequate climbing facilities.

The Rainbow Boa (*Epicrates cenchria*) from South and Central America belongs to a genus more typical of the West Indies. As its popular name indicates, the snake's body is iridescent in the sun. The largest species of the genus *Epicrates*, *Epicrates angulifer*, attains a maximum length of 4.5 m. Its favorite diet consists of

The Emerald or Green Tree Boa, Corallus caninus, *has a reputation as a vicious snake. The front teeth are very long, designed to penetrate the heavy feathers of birds, its main prey. Photo: K. Progsclia.*

The Yellow or Paraguay Anaconda, *Eunectes notaeus*, is smaller and more attractive than the common Anaconda. Photo: B. Kahl.

bats.

Peculiar are the habits of the comparatively small snakes of the genus *Eryx*. Their relatively short body is largely adapted to a life in sandy steppes and semi-arid terrain. Conspicuous are the small eyes and the short tail.

One species belonging to this genus which occurs in Europe as well—it has spread from Asia Minor via western Greece to the Black Sea—is the Sand Boa (*Eryx jaculus*). For this snake the terrarium must have a layer of sand with a depth of at least 20 to 25 cm and the temperature at that level must be kept at 20 to 24°C. The sand-colored snakes spend almost the whole day buried in the sand, with only the eyes and nose protruding. Prey is seized after a sudden forward thrust and killed by constriction. Sand Boas are greedy animals and jealous of one another's food. They feed on mice, lizards, the eggs of reptiles, and slugs.

The Indian Sand Boa (*Eryx johni*) lives in similar steppe terrain. One specimen which spent a total of 18 years in captivity attained a length of 95 cm.

North America is the native range of two boids. The Rosy Boa (*Lichanura trivirgata*) inhabits the oak forests of the California coastal regions east to Arizona and south into northwestern Mexico and feeds on small rodents and nestlings. The bluish gray basic color of the body is interrupted by several pink to reddish brown zigzag or straight bands. Rosy Boas are long-lived and very peaceable pets. As peaceful and harmless is the Rubber Boa (*Charina bottae*). It does not attack even in self-defense but, like *Lichanura trivirgata*, rolls itself up into a ball, with the head in the center, and thus seeks to fend off its enemy or attacker. Unlike the Old World species of the genus

The Indian or Brown Sand Boa, Eryx johni*, is long-lived though not very colorful. Like other sand boas, it is secretive. Photo: J. P. Swaak.*

Eryx, however, the Rubber Boa does not live in arid steppe terrain but prefers the damp coniferous forests of the Pacific Northwest.

The typical pythons comprise some four to five genera, the exact number varying with the authority. The genus *Python* itself extends its range from West Africa over the whole African continent to the southern Sahara. In Asia these snakes occur from India to southern China and throughout Indonesia into New Guinea and Australia. All species lay eggs that in some are incubated by the mother. After producing the eggs, the female coils on top of them and does not stop incubating until just before the young are due to hatch. It was found that in some species the temperature between the coiled portions of the mother's body may be as much as 7°C higher than the atmospheric temperature. In other words, the mother snake genuinely

The subadult of the Indian Sand Boa, Eryx johni, has a banded pattern that darkens to a uniform brown with age. Some subspecies of E. johni retain at least remnants of the banded pattern throughout life. Photo: J. Wines.

incubates the eggs. The latter are left only for brief periods when the snake goes off to drink water.

The largest species of the genus *Python* is the Reticulated Python (*Python reticulatus*), which can

A dark phase Reticulated Python, Python reticulatus. Notice the narrow dark line running the entire length of the top of the head.

Facing page: *The true Indian Python, Python molurus molurus. Note that the dark arrowhead pattern does not extend beyond the eyes. Photo: Cotswold Wildlife Park.*

sometimes exceed 9 m in length. Animals measuring 5 to 7 m are far from rare. The native range of the Reticulated Python extends from southern Burma over the whole of southeastern Asia, including all the larger islands of Indonesia and the Philippines. The basic color is a dirty brown to reddish gray which makes the black net-like pattern with the yellow edges look very conspicuous. The Reticulated Python likes being in water and is an excellent swimmer. Its favorite food consists of whatever fowl is available. In its native regions it frequently ventures into the proximity of human habitations. By day the

The Jamaican Boa, Epicrates subflavus. *Photo: R. D. Bartlett.*

snakes lie inside stacks of wood, in storage places, and similar hiding places. Only at dusk does the search for food begin. Chickens, ducks, cats, dogs, even pigs are said to be overpowered.

The clutch consists of a lumpy heap of 80 eggs or more. Their size ranges from 8 to 10 cm. After leaving the egg membrane a young Reticulated Python has a length of 60 to 75 cm.

A length of a mere 5 m is attained by the "Light Phase" or Indian Python (*Python molurus molurus*) which is native to India and Sri Lanka. On a light brown base it shows a conspicuous pattern of broad, dark brown squares with yellow edges. Its diet consists of mammals, birds, and reptiles. Twelve to 15 weeks elapse between copulation and egg-laying. The number of eggs fluctuates between 10 and 100. The eggs take eight weeks to mature. The larger and darker race of *Python molurus*, *Python*

molurus bivittatus, is commonly referred to as the "Dark Phase" or Burmese Python. The range includes much of Indo-China, southern China, and Indonesia.

Native to the whole of southern and tropical Africa as far north as the southern region of the Sahara is the African Rock Python (*Python sebae*) which grows to a length of 7 m and is thus the largest African snake. This species favors the open plains and savannas above all, although it can sometimes be seen in forests as well. Its diet consists of larger rodents, fowl, small young antelopes, and pigs.

Extremely peaceable and ideal for the terrarium is the Royal Python (*Python regius*). It is native to West Africa and rarely exceeds 2 m in length. When feeling

Facing page: A newborn Cook's Tree Boa, Corallus enydris cookii, from northern South America. Photo: P. J. Stafford.

threatened it rolls itself up into a ball and behaves similarly to some of the boids already described. This affable species is highly recommended to the novice. Closely related to the Royal Python is the Angolan Python (*Python anchietae*) which hails from Angola and grows to about 1 m.

More in need of warmth than all the other pythons is the Blood Python (*Python curtus*) which occurs on the Malaysian peninsula, on Sumatra and Borneo. It owes its popular name to its red coloration which is broken up by black and grayish yellow spots. This snake not only likes the proximity of accumulations of water, of rivers and swamps, but occasionally feeds underwater, i.e., while lying in the water, as well. It is very difficult to keep successfully.

The Australian Carpet or Diamond Python (*Morelia spilotes*) occurs in the coastal regions of Australia

One of the most attractively patterned sand boas is Eryx colubrinus loveridgei, *the Kenyan Sand Boa. Although bred in captivity and available on a regular basis, it tends to be a secretive burrower. Photo: R. T. Zappalorti.*

and New Guinea. The back is adorned with yellow to yellowish green patches of a peculiar, rhombus-like shape. The species favors damp localities and during a dry spell retreats into caves.

In the mangrove forests along the coastal strip of northern Australia lives the splendid Amethystine Python *(Liasis amethystinus)* which attains a length of 6.5 m. This species is seldom kept in the terrarium,

Facing page: A litter of newborn tree boas, Corallus enydris enydris. *This is one of the more variable snakes. Photo: R. A. Winstel.*

Below: Eryx jaculus, *one of the many Asian sand boas that appear on the market occasionally. Photo: C. Banks.*

however. The Green Tree Python (*Chondrophyton viridis*) which is found mostly on New Guinea bears a remarkable resemblance to the Emerald Tree Boa (*Corallus caninus*) from South America. It grows to over 2 m and is bright green in color. A prominent white dorsal line with crossbars that branch off it to both sides is also present.

Calabria reinhardti is a python that lives below ground. It occurs in Liberia

The Rosy Boa, Lichanura trivirgata, *of the* southwestern United States and adjacent Mexico. Photo: I. Francais.

Top: Python anchietae, *the Angolan Python. Photo: K. H. Switak.* **Bottom:** Calabaria reinhardti, *the Burrowing Python. Photo: P. J. Stafford.*

and in the extensive rain forests of the Congo basin. When touched, it rolls itself up into a ball, just like the Rosy Boa and the Royal Python. This brownish red snake with reddish speckles barely reaches a length of 1 m.

BLIND SNAKES
Typhlopids and
Leptotyphlopids

Blind snakes and slender blind snakes are mostly small, burrowing reptiles with a smooth, cylindrical body, a blunt snout and a short tail which sometimes bears a pointed thorn on one of its terminal scales. This thorn borne by what are entirely harmless animals was superstitiously and erroneously described in the past as a poison thorn. It is likely that its function is connected with locomotion underground. The whole body is covered by small, smooth, and shiny scales, including the underside since the blind snakes lack the characteristic broadened ventral scales by means of which other snakes propel themselves. A further peculiarity of the blind snakes is the structure of their skull. Whereas in most snakes the skeleton of the head consists of individual bones which are connected to each other by strands of elastic tissue, many bones that make up the skull of the blind snakes are fused with one another, thereby making the capsule of the skull considerably firmer and more rigid. The skull has, therefore, largely been adapted to the burrowing habits of these animals.

Over 200 species of typhlopids are known, and these are native to Africa, Madagascar, Southeast Asia, Australia, and the American tropics. A single species, the Worm Snake or Balkan Blind Snake *(Typhlops vermicularis)* occurs in southwestern Asia and has also been found in

Europe, i.e., in Greece. The Worm Snake is well suited for keeping in captivity. In the terrarium these animals are fed on a variety of ants and their pupae. Since they burrow, they are virtually vivaparous species, of which *Typhlops diardii* from Southeast Asia is one example.

The family of leptotyphlopids or slender blind snakes embraces a

The Brahminy Blind Snake, Ramphotyphlops braminus, *the only snake known to have been introduced accidentally into the continental United States. Photo: A. Kerstitch.*

never visible at the surface and thus make very dull pets.

Most blind snakes barely exceed 40 cm in length. As a rule they are oviparous, but we also know of a few mere 40 species whose main range of distribution is Africa. Only a few live in tropical America. On an average, the slender blind snakes are even smaller than the typhlopids. The

One of the few interestingly patterned blind snakes, Rhinotyphlops schinzi *from southern Africa. Photo: P. Freed.*

smaller species grow to little more than 10 cm while the largest species do not exceed 30 cm in length.

Blind snakes are rarely kept in the terrarium. With the exception of a few dietary specialists that feed on specific termites, these animals should not in any way be difficult to keep. Very little is known about the habits of these snakes. For this reason, terrarium

The Texas Blind Snake, Leptotyphlops dulcis. *Photo: S. Minton.*

enthusiasts in particular could make valuable observations and give important advice.

BURROWING SNAKES
Aniliidae, Uropeltidae, and Xenopeltidae

The burrowing snakes are non-venomous subterranean snakes with a cylindrical body, a small head, and a short tail.

The first family, the Aniliidae or pipe snakes, forms a small group which, similar to the giant snakes (Boidae), have a vestigial pelvic girdle and vestigial limbs, the latter in the form of claws on either side of the cloaca. One genus is native to South America; the other two genera occur in southeast Asia.

The best known is the

Leptotyphlops humilis *from Arizona. Photo: A. Kerstitch.*

Cylindrophis rufum, *a pipesnake from Asia. Photo: R. D. Bartlett.*

Coral Pipe Snake, *Anilus scytale*, which attains a maximum length of 90 cm and is kept in the terrarium from time to time. Its coloration—a bright red body color interrupted at regular intervals by black crossbands—is similar to that of several venomous coral snakes of the genus Micrurus, except that the yellow crossbands are absent. This snake gives birth to living young and feeds on lizards and smaller snakes.

Native exclusively to southern India and Sri Lanka are the uropeltids or shield-tail snakes, of which some 40 species have been described so far. As the name implies, the greatly enlarged scale at the end of the short tail sometimes has been modified into a shield-like structure. The purpose of this arrangement is to assist with the burrowing, like the terminal thorn on the tail of typhlopids. Shield-tail snakes are livebearers and give birth to about three to eight young at a time. Most species remain small and rarely grow longer than 30 cm. The bulk of their diet consists of earthworms and the larvae of insects.

The xenopeltids or sunbeam snakes occur in Southeast Asia. The only species seen on occasion, *Xenopeltis unicolor*, reaches a length of up to 1 m. The head is slightly broadened and therefore distinct from the body. The deep brown back is iridescent. The underside is white in color. By night the snake leaves its burrow and surfaces in search of food. Its diet is composed of frogs, lizards, small mammals, and birds. One specimen is known to have lived in captivity for 15 years.

Where burrowing snakes are to be kept, the interior of the terrarium must be adapted to the animals' habits. The bottom should be covered with a loosely packed mixture of soil and leaves to a minimum depth of 15 to 20 cm so that ample digging and burrowing facilities are available.

Xenopeltis unicolor, *the Sunbeam Snake. Photo: S. Minton.*

TYPICAL SNAKES
Colubridae

The family of colubrids or "typical snakes" embraces about 270 genera. Of these, about 70 genera belong to the rear-fanged colubrids or Boiginae, while the remaining genera are dispersed among 10-20 other poorly defined subfamilies. Even the Boiginae is now considered to be an artificial group used strictly for convenience.

The teeth of the Colubrinae or "typical snakes" in the stricter sense (including all the subfamilies but Boiginae) show no grooves. The same does not apply where the Boiginae are concerned. Here the upper teeth toward the rear of the mouth have a groove by means of which the venom is conveyed into the bite wound of the prey. This poison is produced inside the salivary gland of virtually all "typical snakes," including those in which a direct exit and a connection

A Ringneck Snake, Diadophis punctatus, *exhibiting both the ring on the neck and the brightly colored ventral surface. Photo: J. Iverson.*

The Smooth Snake, Coronella austriaca, *is more or less the European equivalent of a North American kingsnake. Popular pets, they often are protected by law. Photo: S. Kochetov.*

with the jaw are absent. Even in the Grass Snake (*Natrix natrix*) certain parts of the salivary gland produce a poisonous secretion, and serious bites by such harmless species as the Eastern Hognose are on record.

Many species among the colubrids can be regarded as modified forms that have been adapted to certain habitats and consequently show anatomical or biological peculiarities. The ecological group with the greatest number of species consists of the ground-dwelling snakes that are hardly modified at all. In addition, there are digging and burrowing species with a short tail and a blunt head, arboreal snakes with a long, pointed head and an extended, prehensile tail and, finally, highly aquatic water snakes.

A classic representative of the non-specialized ground-dwelling snakes is the Smooth Snake (*Coronella austriaca*). It grows to a length of about 60 to 70 cm. The brown background color is more reddish in the males and predominantly grayish brown in the females. Extending along the back there is a row of dark spots. These sometimes merge into a zigzag band and often cause frightened and uninformed people to kill the harmless snake, mistaking it for an Adder. Characteristic is the dark stripe between the nostril and the corner of the mouth. The scales, as the name implies, are smooth and not keeled. In the male the scales on the underside are yellowish red whereas in females they are grayish red in color.

Coronella austriaca is excellently suited for the terrarium. Although this species is a pronounced ground-dweller, some animals turn out to be extraordinarily agile climbers in the terrarium. In their natural habitat they like to sunbathe on flat boulders and old walls.

After quickly seizing the prey, the snake wraps itself around it. The diet is composed mostly of Sand Lizards (*Lacerta agilis*) and Slowworms (*Anguis fragilis*). Occasionally, young snakes, small rodents, birds, and lizard's eggs are devoured as well. More rarely, the species will take crickets, grasshoppers, slugs, and earthworms.

The natural habitat of the Smooth Snake consists of open, dry, and sunny

Coluber jugularis, a Eurasian racer.
Photo: B. Kahl.

terrain with warm spots, heaps of stones, clearings, and holes in the ground. The range of distribution extends from France to the Caspian Sea, southward as far as Sicily and the Balkans. The species also occurs in southern Britain.

After mating in the spring (the winter quarters are left in mid-April) the female produces two to fifteen young between the end of August and the beginning of October. The young snakes leave the egg membranes immediately after they are born. In the early stages they feed on earthworms, mealworms, slugs, and smooth caterpillars, later on young lizards and young Slowworms. Often they also devour the weaker ones of their own siblings.

Very closely related to this species is *Coronella girondica*, the Southern Smooth Snake, which is native to the southern Tyrol, Italy, southwestern Europe, and northwest Africa. This snake loves a dry climate and is active at dusk. It, too, is well suited for the terrarium.

Aesculapian Snakes *(Elaphe longissima)* grow to a length of up to 2 m and live in open deciduous forests with sunny meadows and heaps of stones. The snake, which moves smoothly and elegantly, seeks refuge inside hollow tree trunks or in old walls. It is not only on the ground, however, that its agility is in evidence; the snake is an excellent climber as well. By wedging the edges of its ventral scales into cracks in the bark it is able to climb up high trees in order to rest and sun itself among the branches. Perpendicular walls and rock faces are successfully negotiated, too.

Because of the yellowish spots situated behind the head on each side, the Aesculapian Snake is frequently confused with the Grass Snake. What distinguishes the two,

The Eurasian Four-lined Snake, Elaphe quatuorlineata. *Photo: B. Kahl.*

The Aesculapian Snake, Elaphe longissima, *a European rat snake. Photo: B. Kahl.*

however, is that the deep brown dorsal scales of the former, which are adorned with white lines, are smooth and unkeeled. The diet consists of mice, birds, and birds' eggs. Lizards are eaten only by young animals. Generally speaking, the clutch comprises five to eight eggs from which the young snakes emerge after 50 to 60 days, measuring 17 to 20 cm in length.

This species must be kept in large terraria with firm shrubs and a water basin which is shallow but spacious.

Equally spacious terraria with strong branches for climbing and a large water basin are required for keeping the Four-lined Snake (*Elaphe quatuorlineata*). On the top side this snake is brown in color. Characteristic are the four longitudinal stripes and the black band on the forehead. The snake attains a length of up to 2.5 m and a maximum thickness of 10 cm. It occurs naturally in Italy, southern Istria, Dalmatia, and Greece. In Turkey, southern Russia, and Asia Minor we find the subspecies *Elaphe quatuorlineata sauromates*.

Four-lined Snakes remain loyal to one locality and sometimes live in deep holes in the ground. Their movements are deliberate and slow. If the snake suddenly finds itself threatened, it makes no attempt to escape, strangely enough, but hisses and rolls itself up. It never makes any hasty movements to defend itself. Even when touched it seldom bites.

The food requirements of the Four-lined Snake are considerable. Young animals live mainly on lizards. Adult animals, on the other hand, feed on guinea pigs, rats, newly-born hares, moles and mice. They also take birds and birds' eggs.

Magnificent in color is the Leopard Snake (*Elaphe*

The Yellow Rat Snake of the southeastern United States, Elaphe obsoleta quadrivittata. *Photo: R. Everhart.*

In North America, members of the genus Coluber *are called racers, while in Europe they are called whip snakes. This is the Eurasian* Coluber jugularis. *Photo: B. Kahl.*

markings and there is a big horseshoe-shaped patch on the nape. The range of distribution extends from southern Italy to the Crimean peninsula. The diet consists predominantly of mice. The eggs are

situla). The deep brown to blood red spots with their black borders contrast beautifully with the grayish yellow background color. The head shows black comparatively large and the young animals measure from 31 to 35 cm in length when they hatch.

The Ladder Snake (*Elaphe scalaris*) is native to

southern France and the Pyrenees. It attains an average length of 1.50 m, although larger specimens have on occasion been recorded from Spain. The brownish yellow to olivaceous back is adorned with two black longitudinal lines. The underside is uniformly yellow. Ladder Snakes favor dry hedges and vineyards.

Closely related to each other are the Balkan Whip Snake (*Coluber gemonensis*),

The Leopard Snake, Elaphe situla, *is considered one of the most desirable of Eurasian species. Photo: K. Knaack.*

The Cowl Snake, Macroprotodon cucullatus, *of southwestern Europe and northern Africa is one of the few rear-fanged species that enters Europe. Photo: K. H. Switak.*

the Western Whip Snake (*Coluber viridiflavus*), and *Coluber jugularis caspius*. In the past these animals, now classified as species in their own right, were regarded as subspecies of *Coluber gemonensis*. All of them favor rocky, dry terraria with spacious water containers. The most handsome of this tribe is the Western Whip Snake. It grows up to 1.80 m long. The dorsal side is black—covered in greenish yellow speckles anteriorly. The underside tends to be of a dirty gray coloration and in many cases every ventral shield bears a dark lateral spot. This snake is widespread in southwestern Europe, southern Switzerland, Italy, on Corsica and Sardinia. The favorite food consists of lizards.

Two snakes which should be kept in dry terraria and likewise feed almost exclusively on lizards are Dahl's or the Slender Whip Snake (*Coluber najadum*) and the Horseshoe Snake (*Coluber hippocrepis*). The latter lives in the western Mediterranean region and the horseshoe-shaped pattern on the top of the head makes it unmistakable. The body is blackish, with numerous dark rings and spots.

The three European rear-fanged colubrids (opisthoglyphs), the Montpellier Snake (*Malpolon monspessulanus*), the Cowl Snake (*Macroprotodon cucullatus*), and the Cat Snake (*Telescopus fallax*), hail from North Africa and southwestern Asia. Via the Balkans, Spain, and Sicily they entered the European range so that the Cat Snake and one race of the Montpellier Snake (*Malpolon monspessulanus insignitus*) are now found on the Balkan peninsula while the Cowl Snake and the *Malpolon monspessulanus* occur on the Pyrenean peninsula.

The Montpellier Snake

needs large, spacious containers and is very voracious. Lizards, great and small, as well as snakes and anguids are pursued with the mouth partially open. In captivity it remains very shy and often does not go near the food until many weeks of acclimatization have passed. Its venom is unlikely to be especially harmful to humans, although individual cases of severe poisoning have been described in the literature.

The Cat Snake's venom is of no significance to human beings either. Frequently it is only sufficient to kill the first food animal, subsequent ones being killed by constriction.

Widespread on the African continent is the Hissing Sand Snake (*Psammophis sibilans*). It occurs on open grass and scrub land as well as in cultivated regions and near rivers. *Psammophis sibilans* is strictly diurnal and feeds on frogs, toads, lizards,

birds, and smaller mammals.

Boaedon lineatus, the Striped House Snake, ventures near human habitations even more than the Hissing Sand Snake. This brown snake has been encountered beneath rugs, compost heaps, and even in gutters. The harmless animal, which makes itself very useful inside houses and outbuildings by eliminating mice, rarely grows to more than 1 m in length. The reddish brown back is sometimes covered with yellowish speckles.

The species *Crotaphopeltis hotamboeia*, the White-lipped Snake, an opisthoglyph, originates from tropical and southern Africa. The bulk of its diet consists of toads and frogs, which is why it favors the proximity of stagnant or slow-flowing waters.

The magnificent *Telescopus semiannulatus* from East and South Africa attains a length of about 1

Even though most specimens have bright red upper lips, the African Crotaphopeltis hotamboeia *often is called the White-lipped Snake. Photo: K. H. Switak.*

m. On a yellowish brown background the snake shows a pattern of conspicuous black saddle spots. It feeds almost exclusively on lizards.

Very hardy and prolific in the terrarium—a female can give birth to as many as 80 young—is the grayish brown

Mole Snake (*Pseudaspis cana*). Its favorite food consists of rodents. The species inhabits the arid regions from Angola via the Congo to South Africa.

The sand-colored, dark spotted *Spalerosophis diadema* lives in the semi-arid regions and on the scree slopes of Egypt and the rest of North Africa. It grows to a length of up to 1.80 m. Because of its delicate constitution, it is not advisable to keep this snake in the terrarium.

The Egg-eating Snake (*Dasypeltis scabra*) which occurs naturally from southern East Africa to the Cape is an extreme dietary specialist. As a result of its peculiar diet, this species has lost its dentition, apart from a few vestigial teeth. It feeds exclusively on birds' eggs which it engulfs after spreading its jaws to quite unbelievable proportions. The eggshells are sawed through by means of spinous extensions of the anterior neck vertebrae which project into the gullet and are described as pharyngeal "teeth." As the undamaged egg slides down, these processes are pushed downward to break the shell. The latter is regurgitated shortly after, still hanging together.

Among the more frequently seen ground-dwelling snakes from Asia are *Elaphe dione*, light reddish brown to pale gray, with dark spots, up to 1 m long; the Indian Ratsnake (*Ptyas mucosus*); and *Lycodon aulicus*.

Elaphe dione is a typical ground-dweller and lives mostly in grassy steppes and salt plains. This species often is encountered near rivers and in the vicinity of farms where, after dark, it hunts for food animals such as lizards, snakes, frogs, and toads, and sometimes birds and small mammals as well.

One of the most beautiful of the North American

The Egg-eating Snake or Common Eggeater, Dasypeltis scabra. *Photos: A. van den Nieuwenhuizen.*

snakes is the Corn Snake (*Elaphe guttata*). It goes hunting for mice in the extensive cereal fields of large farms. This snake, reddish brown and adorned with crimson spots that have a black border, is active at dusk and comes out of hiding only toward nightfall. It grows very tame and has been successfully

Africa and the Near East are home to many species of sand snakes, genus Psammophis. *This is* Psammophis leightoni namibensis *from Namibia. Photo: P. Freed.*

bred in the terrarium on a number of occasions.

The natural range of the Fox Snake (*Elaphe vulpina*) extends from northern Wisconsin to Nebraska. This species generally grows to a length of 1.50 m. It is an excellent rat-catcher and, when attacked, instantly assumes a threat and defensive posture, with its tail shaking violently. The rustling noise caused in this way, especially when the animal crawls through fallen leaves, often results in its being mistaken for a rattlesnake.

The common and widespread Eastern Rat Snake *(Elaphe obsoleta)* is found in various subspecies and color patterns through all of the eastern United States. It feeds on birds and their eggs as well as rats and mice. In the subspecies *quadrivittata* four light brown longitudinal stripes extend over the whole body. The Black Rat Snake *(E. o. obsoleta)* is solid dusky black in the adult and grows to more than 1.80 m long.

The snakes of the genus *Pituophis* virtually live underground. Among them, the Bull Snake (*Pituophis catenifer*) is best suited for the terrarium. It is yellowish brown in color and covered in irregular black or reddish brown spots. A dry and warm bottom layer is essential if the species is to be kept successfully.

Very popular in the terrarium are the North American kingsnakes of the genus *Lampropeltis*. The Milk Snake (*Lampropeltis triangulum*)—legend has it that it goes into barns and drinks milk from the cows' udders—is found all over the North American continent into northwestern South America. The Eastern Kingsnake (*Lampropeltis getulus*), of which many different subspecies exist showing a wide variety of colors, occurs all across the continent from New Jersey to California into Mexico.

Telescopus semiannulatus, *often called the Cat Snake, is a rear-fanged lizard-eater of Africa. Photo: H. Nicolay.*

The stem form, *Lampropeltis getulus getulus,* is found more in the Atlantic coastal region and is distinguished by a chain-like pattern of yellow and black. In the Mississippi basin lives the Speckled Kingsnake (*Lampropeltis getulus holbrooki*), which shows yellow speckles on a greenish base. On account of its color pattern the most beautiful kingsnake is the California Mountain Kingsnake (*Lampropeltis zonata*) which, similar to the coral snakes, is adorned with rings of white, black, and red.

Since the kingsnakes, whose average size is between 1 m and 1.5 m, adapt readily to pink mice, they are excellent terrarium animals.

The Racer (*Coluber constrictor*) lives over much of the United States and occurs in many colors, from shiny black to bright blue or even speckled. The pale gray young snakes have brown spots on the back and black speckles on the flanks. This species favors fields and roadsides with sunny edges and plenty of shrubs and attains a length of over 2 m. Eight to 25 white eggs are laid around June and the young snakes hatch eight to ten weeks later, measuring 20 to 30 cm in length.

One of the most attractive of the North American ground-dwelling snakes is the Eastern Indigo Snake (*Drymarchon corais couperi*). The range of the species (most of the other subspecies are tan with black spots) extends into South America, but this subspecies is almost restricted to Florida and Georgia. Its shiny bluish black coloration, changing into many different shades of color on the glistening underside, is magnificent. The Indigo Snake is fairly hardy in the terrarium and not unduly susceptible to disease, nor does it make any special demands as

A litter of albino and normal hatchlings of the Corn Snake, Elaphe guttata. *Photo: K. T. Nemuras.*

regards nutrition, eating small mammals, birds, lizards, frogs, and even venomous snakes.

Threatening and frightening to look at are the hognosed snakes, of which a total of three species are known. They owe their popular name to the upturned snout which looks vaguely like a pig's nose. Their peculiar defensive behavior is of interest. If a hognosed snake suddenly finds itself attacked, its first reaction is to puff itself up to such an extent that it doubles or trebles in circumference. At the same time it repeatedly strikes at its foe, but without actually biting, and gives vent to an audible hiss. Eventually, if these threatening gestures remain ineffective, the molested animal contorts, throws itself onto its back, and shams death. The snake remains in this position even when touched. If turned over, however, it immediately rolls over on its back again. After a few minutes, when all danger is past, the snake cautiously lifts its head, flicks with the tongue, and slowly crawls away.

The Southern Hognosed Snake (*Heterodon simus*), which attains a length of 50 to 60 cm, occurs from North Carolina to Mississippi. The most familiar species, the Eastern Hognosed Snake (*Heterodon platyrhinos*), occurs over much of the eastern United States and feeds almost exclusively on toads. Finally, the Western Hognosed Snake (*Heterodon nasicus*), which has a particularly prominent "snout," occurs in the Great Plains from Canada to Mexico. It takes lizards readily, so it is more amenable to captivity than the other species. The small burrowing snakes of the genus *Chionactis*, which grow to about 45 cm, are native to the desert regions of the southwestern USA and northwestern Mexico.

Dasypeltis scabra, *the most commonly seen egg-eating snake.* Photo: W. B. Allen, Jr.

These charmingly colored snakes with pink, yellow, and black rings are insectivores and need to be kept in dry, sandy terraria with a high ground temperature. They usually fare poorly in captivity.

Below: *An Eastern Hognosed Snake,* Heterodon platyrhinos, *feigning death. Photo: J. Dommers.* **Facing page:** *Florida Kingsnake,* Lampropeltis getulus floridana. *Photo: K. T. Nemuras.*

An Eastern Hognosed Snake swallowing a toad, its normal food. Photo: R. T. Zappalorti.

In recent years the Banded Cat-eyed Snake (*Leptodeira annulata*) has very often been brought to Germany with fruit imports. Hidden inside bunches of bananas in particular (hence its German popular name "Banana Snake"), it gets into the wholesalers' storage areas. Provided the animals arrive without a spinal injury and without open wounds, they quickly acclimatize and are quite hardy. A *Leptodeira annulata* adopted by the author, for example, started feeding inside the terrarium within a few hours of its arrival. Four Edible Frogs (*Rana esculenta*) of medium size were consumed within an hour.

The last ground-dwelling snake to be mentioned here is the ophiophagous, i.e., snake-eating, Mussurana (*Clelia clelia*), which is able to devour highly poisonous viperids and crotalids. Apart from a whitish longitudinal

A young Gray-banded Kingsnake, Lampropeltis alterna. *Photo: A. Kerstitch.*

A Fox Snake, Elaphe vulpina, *one of the more distinctive rat snakes. The species is found mostly around the Great Lakes of the United States and Canada. Photo: R. Everhart.*

One of the most variable North American snakes is the Racer, Coluber
constrictor. *This is one of the blue subspecies,* C. c. foxi, *from the Midwest.
Photo: J. K. Langhammer.*

band, the animals are bluish black all over. Their maximum length is 2 m. They are unsuitable for the terrarium.

The genus *Elaphe*, which belongs to the ground-dwelling snakes, includes a few forms which are not only excellent climbers but actually spend the whole day among branches and in trees. The true tree snakes (unfortunately this categorization is a difficult one to make in some cases) conquered the scrub and shrubs, branches and treetops as their habitat. The majority of them have a slender, elongated body and a long tail. With elegant movements they creep or hurry through the twigs, and, loosely coiled, they hang among the branches, resting and basking in the sun.

The great majority

Above: Leptodeira nigrofasciata, *one of the Central American cat-eyed snakes or "banana snakes."* Photo: P. Freed. **Facing page:** *A Mussurana,* Clelia clelia, *in the steel-gray phase.* Photo: M. Freiberg.

of tree snakes originate in the tropics and must, therefore, be kept in rain-forest terraria at a temperature of 25 to 30°C and an atmospheric humidity of 60 to 70%.

An arboreal snake which belongs to the opisthoglyphs is *Dendrelaphis picta*. This bronze-colored species, which grows to an average length of 1 m, is native to India, Sri Lanka, the Sundas, Philippines, and Moluccas. It favors open terrain, rich in scrub. At night it keeps to the ground. The diet consists of frogs.

Another opisthoglyph is the well-known *Ahaetulla nasuta*, a typical tree snake with a projection at the tip of the upper jaw and a long, whip-like body. On the ground its movements are clumsy and slow. This species is magnificent in color—bluish green to yellowish brown with a yellowish white line on the ventral edges. A striking characteristic is the shape of the pupil—like a horizontal key-hole. This peculiarity appears to be connected with the way the snake procures its food. After making an abrupt lunge with the anterior part of the body, the snake seizes its prey—lizards and treefrogs—immediately behind the head and sometimes, if the effect of the venom is not enough to kill them, swallows them when they are still wriggling. *Ahaetulla nasuta* is a livebearer.

Highly remarkable are the flying snakes of the genus *Chrysopelea*. The species of this genus are distributed over Southeast Asia and India. These snakes are able to glide from the higher branches to the lower ones by a sudden launching of the body during which they

Ahaetulla prasina, *one of the long-nosed tree snakes of tropical Asia. This genus has the horizontal figure-eight pupil seen in several vine snakes. Photo: B. Kahl.*

draw in their under-surface until it is concave. The best known representative of the genus is the Flying Snake (*Chrysopelea ornata*). The

Sloughing takes place every 45 days. In captivity it feeds on lizards,

The Mangrove Snake (*Boiga dendrophila*) has the

The Mangrove Snake, Boiga dendrophila, *is one of the most beautiful snakes, but unfortunately it also is a very dangerous rear-fang that can cause serious injuries and possibly even death. Photo: B. Kahl.*

coloration of these appealing tree snakes shows a great deal of individual variation. Black, yellow, yellowish red, and green shades of color vary, depending on locality.

same range of distribution. The generic name *Boiga* was adopted for the rear-fanged colubrids as a whole (Boiginae). The Malays refer to this large-eyed nocturnal snake as "Ularburong." The upper parts of the snake are deep black in color. On the flanks, at wide intervals, there are narrow yellow stripes. The scales on the snout and upper lip are yellow as well. This species feeds on lizards, snakes, and birds, after killing them by means of its comparatively fast-acting venom. A close relative, *Boiga trigonata*, is a nutritional specialist. It favors agamids of the genus *Calotes*.

The Flying Snake, Chrysopelea ornata, *another rear-fanged species. Photo: B. Kahl.*

The only rear-fanged snake that is consistently deadly to human beings is the Boomslang (*Dispholidus typus*) native to equatorial and southern Africa. Often this green, slender scrub- and tree-dwelling snake lies inside birds' nests after having devoured their contents, both young birds and eggs. In addition, the species favors chameleons.

The emerald green *Leptophis mexicanus* hails from Mexico and Central America. It rarely exceeds 100 cm in length and its diet consists of lizards and frogs. Distributed over northern South America is *Leptophis ahaetulla*, which attains a maximum length of 1.20 m and is slender and extremely agile. It feeds exclusively on lizards.

On the island of Haiti, in

the coconut forests near the shore, live the arboreal snakes *Uromacer catesbyi* and *Uromacer oxyrhynchus*. These snakes are infrequently imported. Their natural food is treefrogs,

A young Boomslang, Dispholidus typus. Photo: J. Visser.

and *U. oxyrhynchus* also eats lizards of the genus *Anolis*.

In Brazil, *Spilotes pullatus* is often kept as a house snake to control the vast numbers of mice and rats. In its natural environment the species favors scrub and shrubs in the proximity of water.

Of the vine snakes (genus *Oxybelis*) native to the American tropics, the two better known species shall be mentioned here. They show the color scheme common to many arboreal snakes: *Oxybelis fulgidis* is bright green with one whitish longitudinal stripe on each flank while *Oxybelis aeneus* is the color of brown bark.

Tomodon dorsatus is a livebearer. In a terrarium densely planted with *Ficus* and *Philodendron* one female, 80 cm in length, may produce nine young snakes which feed on slugs to start with.

Many species of snakes are known to consume slugs and snails as part of their diet, the young of *Tomodon dorsatus* just mentioned being one example. The slug-eating snakes (genus *Dipsas*), however, actually specialize in this type of food. Their range of distribution extends from southern Mexico to northern Argentina. *Dipsas albifrons*, *Dipsas mikani*, and *Dipsas turgidus* are nocturnal animals which eat both slugs and snails. The shell is removed as a rule and only the soft parts are eaten.

The last ecological group of typical snakes is the water snakes, comprising both aglyphs and opisthoglyphs, which either live in the immediate vicinity of water or actually lead a completely aquatic life and only leave the water to lay eggs. It is essential, therefore, when setting up a terrarium for water snakes, to provide a water basin which is big enough for the snakes to swim in. Completely dry areas must also be created, however. Virtually all water snakes are suitable for the novice since they are hardy, undemanding, and have a good appetite. Obtaining food for them presents no problem either, since frogs, newts, and fish are almost always accepted.

The most common Eurasian natricine snake, the Grass or Ringed Snake (*Natrix natrix natrix*), belongs to the water snakes. (Natricinae is the subfamily of typical water snakes.) It owes its name to the conspicuous and characteristic ring-shaped pattern consisting of two bright yellow semi-lunar patches immediately behind the head. In a few individuals the lunar patches are pale or

completely absent. These markings also show specific variations in the different geographical races. Especially at higher altitudes are found specimens that have lost their lunar patches entirely and are of one color (sometimes black) all over. The upper parts may be gray or steel-colored— sometimes with a greenish and bluish tinge—with or without four to six longitudinal rows of small black or blackish brown specks. Rarely encountered are animals with two light-colored longitudinal rows on the back. These striations are typical for *Natrix natrix persa*, whose main range of distribution is on the southern coast of the Caspian Sea whence it spread into Asia Minor and

An American vine snake, Oxybelis fulgidus. *Note that the pupil is round, not horizontal, in this genus. Photo: K. T. Nemuras.*

One of the more variable Eurasian snakes is the Grass Snake, Natrix natrix. *Melanistic individuals and populations occur in many parts of its wide range. The Grass Snake is closer to a garter snake in captive requirements than to a water snake.*

the Balkan Countries.

Slightly longer than the nominate form of the Grass Snake (*Natrix natrix natrix*), which occurs all over Europe, is the Barred Grass Snake (*Natrix natrix helvetica*), whose range is confined to western and central Europe. In this snake the dark dorsal patches have expanded laterally and changed into bars and the yellow lunar patches are either completely absent or of a pale whitish yellow color.

Detail of the head pattern of a well-marked Grass Snake. Photo: Dr. D. Terver, Nancy Aquarium, France.

Other subspecies are *Natrix natrix sicula*, from Sicily, in which the tip of the snout is yellowish red, *Natrix natrix corsica* from Corsica, and *Natrix natrix cetti* from Sardinia. On the Pyrenean peninsula and in Morocco and Algiers lives *Natrix natrix astreptophora*, and on the Cyclades the small *Natrix natrix schweizeri* which does not usually exceed 60 to 70 cm in length.

Grass Snakes are excellent swimmers and favor the proximity of ditches, bogs, and stagnant and slow-flowing water. They are accommodated in spacious aquaterraria which should include a dry terrestrial area. In elegant undulating movements, with the head raised, they swim through the water. Now and then they dive to considerable depths, being able to comb the bottom for food for minutes at a time. The diet consists of frogs,

Natrix natrix helvetica, the Barred Grass Snake. Photo: B. Kahl.

newts, fish, and tadpoles. Above all, they like treefrogs. Toads and fire salamanders are avoided because of the dermal secretions of these amphibians.

The Viperine Snake, Natrix maura, *is more aquatic than the Grass Snake and has a smaller range. Photo: B. Kahl.*

In Germany the Grass Snake seldom grows to more than 1 m long. In southern European countries, on the other hand, it can attain a length of up to 1.50 m.

The eggs are laid in July. Eleven to 25 large white eggs are deposited in a grapelike clump among leaves, in compost heaps, or in stables or barns. After seven to ten weeks the young snakes, measuring 15 to 18 cm in length, leave the egg. They feed on the larvae of amphibians and tiny, newly-metamorphosed frogs. Often the adult animals mate again in the fall and the resultant eggs are laid when the female comes out of hibernation. Sexual maturity is attained when the Grass Snakes are 60 cm long and about three to four

One of the most common water snakes of the southern United States is the Banded Water Snake, Nerodia fasciata. *The American water snakes give live birth, while the Eurasian water snakes usually lay eggs. Photo: R. Anderson.*

years old. Breeding in the terrarium succeeds regularly once the pairs have become acclimatized. The snakes move into their winter quarters toward the end of September or the beginning of October.

Even more dependent on an aquatic environment than the Grass Snake is the Tessellated Snake (*Natrix tessellata*), and the same applies where the Viperine

Snake (*Natrix maura*) from southwestern Europe is concerned. Both spend nearly their whole life in water or its immediate proximity, On the yellowish brown to olive back the Tessellated Snake has a row of dark spots. The underside shows a pattern of brownish red and black squares. Its food consists mainly of fish. The range of the Viperine Snake lies in the Rhone

Above: Rhabdophis subminiatus *(formerly in the genus* Natrix*) of southern Asia has enlarged rear teeth and may be dangerous. Photo: R. D. Bartlett.* ***Facing page:*** *The Tiger Water Snake,* Rhabdophis *(formerly* Natrix*)* tigrinus*, has caused one or two human deaths. Photo: S. Kochetov.*

region of Switzerland south to northwestern Africa. Characteristic are dark eye spots with a light nucleus which extend along the flanks. The food animals are engulfed alive as is the prey of the Tessellated Snake. In addition to fish, the Viperine Snake feeds on earthworms, water shrews, and frogs.

As widespread and common as *Natrix* is in Europe are the *Nerodia* (livebearing water snakes) in North America. Among these, the Northern Water Snake (*Nerodia sipedon*) enjoys the widest range of distribution. It extends from southern Canada to the Carolinas and Louisiana, and in the west as far as Colorado. In the southern U.S.A., from Virginia to the Gulf of Mexico and north to Illinois, lives *Nerodia fasciata*. The back of this snake is covered with light and dark crossbands; on the underside it is yellowish with reddish spots.

A little more adapted to aquatic life is *Nerodia fasciata compressicauda*, found in the mangrove thickets of the coastal regions of southern Florida and Cuba. Its slightly vertically flattened tail is unique in the genus. Found through much of the eastern USA are the subspecies of *Nerodia erythrogaster*, with forms extending into Mexico.

The small crayfish-eating Queen Snake *(Nerodia (Regina) septemvittata)* and its relatives are restricted to the eastern USA and adjacent Canada.

The Brown Water Snake, *Nerodia taxispilota,* is the largest North American *Nerodia* species. It grows over 1.5 m long. This dirty brown snake, with a chain of black spots across its back, not only sprays a foul-smelling liquid from its cloacal glands—as do nearly all the natricine snakes when molested or touched—but puffs itself up during an attack, flattens the head, and all too readily administers a powerful bite. It feeds upon fish and frogs. The prey is devoured underwater. Its favored localities are flooded hollows in the river bank.

Found from Pakistan through much of the Indo-Australian Archipelago is *Natrix (Xenochrophis) piscator,* the Fish Snake, which grows over 1 m long.

On a yellowish brown base it has longitudinal rows of dark spots which often run into each other and conceal the basic color. Its defensive behavior toward enemies is identical to that adopted by *Nerodia taxispilota.*

Described as venomous is *Natrix (Amphiesma) stolata.* Its native range covers India, Sri Lanka, Thailand, and Indo-China. Although this snake, like all species of the genus *Natrix,* does not actually possess specialized teeth for delivering venom, it still manages to inject highly effective venomous secretions into the wound of its prey with its bite.

Natrix (Rhabdophis) tigrina from East Asia adapts well to a life in the terrarium. It is voracious and long-lived and, above all, not too sensitive to low temperatures. This species has black spots on a light gray base. It has occasionally caused venom reactions in humans and thus should be handled

The most common and widely distributed species of North American garter snake, Thamnophis sirtalis. *Photo: B. Kahl.*

carefully.

In North America, the genus of natricine with the greatest number of species is *Thamnophis* (garter snakes). In their behavior and habits these snakes differ only a little from the related European species of the genus *Natrix*. Unlike the latter, however, they are not oviparous but give birth to living young, often a considerable number of them. Their diet consists of fish and amphibians and their larvae. Earthworms and pieces of fish are also accepted. The differentiation and taxonomic arrangement of the individual species is extremely difficult.

Garter snakes are distributed over the whole of the North American continent. In the north, a number of *Thamnophis* species also occur in the Canadian provinces, and in the south they extend their range to as far as Costa Rica.

The most common species is *Thamnophis sirtalis*, a species of which many different subspecies have been described. Characteristic are three prominent yellowish longitudinal stripes on a dark background. At hibernation time numerous animals often get together and move into communal winter quarters (hibernaculum). The delightful young snakes—it is perfectly possible to breed this species in the terrarium and several reports on their propagation in captivity already exist—are raised on earthworms without any difficulties.

Further south, in Argentina and Brazil, there occurs *Leimadophis poecilogyrus*. Dark red cross bands contrast with the background color—yellowish green with an element of black. The underside is brick red. The bright red color of the skin is also in evidence when the scales move apart.

The brightly colored San Francisco Garter Snake, Thamnophis sirtalis tetrataenia, is considered to be endangered because of loss of habitat. Photo: K. Lucas.

Another species that is native to Brazil is *Liophis miliaris*. A striking characteristic of this aquatic snake, which grows to a length of 75 cm, is the black scales with their golden yellow edges.

Farancia erytrogramma (the Rainbow Snake) and the Mud Snake (*Farancia abacura*) live in the southeastern region of the United States. The former is of an exceptionally beautiful and attractive coloration. Three red longitudinal stripes extend along the back and there is another one on each flank. The underside is red and adorned with a longitudinal double row of dark spots. In captivity, the Rainbow Snake feeds on elongated fishes and salamanders. One remarkable characteristic of the Mud Snake is its great proliferation. Up to 104 eggs are laid, but this probably represents a communal nest.

The species of the genus *Dinodon* are confined to Asia and occur from southern China to Manchuria as well as in Taiwan and Japan

A gorgeous juvenile Rainbow Snake, Farancia erytrogramma, *one of the most striking patterned snakes of the southeastern United States. Photo: J. Iverson.*

south to Burma and Vietnam. The back fangs in the upper jaw are greatly enlarged. The best known species is *Dinodon rufozonatum*. All species of this genus are nocturnal.

The piscivorous snakes of the genus *Helicops* live in South American waters. In these snakes the snout looks foreshortened, the eyes are far forward, and the nostrils stand close together on the top of the snout. The diet consists exclusively of fish.

A subfamily of the colubrids is formed by the Indo-Malay-Australian rear-fanged water snakes or Homalopsinae. All of them are opisthoglyphs and all of them are viviparous. The nostrils are situated on the upper parts of the snout and, in adaptation to the aquatic way of life, can be closed by means of valves. The natural diet of these snakes consists of frogs and fish. A few species, such as *Fordonia leucobalia* and

Dinodon rufozonatum, *one of the more interesting species of a large southern Asian genus. Photo: R. E. Kuntz.*

Homalopsis buccata, prefer prawns and other crustaceans.

The rather strange Tentacled Fishing Snake (*Erpeton tentaculatum*), native to Southeast Asia, also belongs to the Homalopsinae. It owes its name to two feeler-like appendages, formed from scales, on the end of the snout. This snake never leaves the water and feeds exclusively on fish.

Below: The Tentacled Snake, Erpeton tentaculatum, *is one of the most distinctive of snakes. It is almost strictly aquatic. Photo: K. H. Switak.*

COBRAS AND THEIR ALLIES

Elapidae

With the Elapidae we come to the venomous snakes in the stricter sense. The elapids or cobras and their allies, the Hydrophiidae or sea snakes, are proteroglyphs. That is, the poison teeth in the anterior part of the upper jaw are equipped with a vertical poison groove; the teeth are fixed and cannot be raised when the bite is administered. Since sea snakes are not suitable for the terrarium, a description of this specialized snake family will be omitted here.

Very different from the poison teeth of the proteroglyphs are those of the solenoglyphs; the latter are far more dangerous throughout. The poison fang of a solenoglyph is folded back when not in use, has a poison canal running through it, and is raised for the bite. The viperids or vipers and the crotalids or pit vipers belong to the solenoglyphs.

Among the elapids we get both extraordinarily dangerous large forms, such as the species of the genus *Naja*, and small species barely growing 40 cm long, whose poisonous bite is no more dangerous than a wasp sting.

None of the elapids are represented in Europe. In North Africa, however, there occurs the famous light to dark brown Egyptian Cobra (*Naja haje*), an elapid known to the ancient Egyptians. In that distant past the snake was regarded as the symbol of powerful rulership and adorned the headdress of the pharaohs. Cleopatra is said to have committed suicide by subjecting herself to the bite of an Egyptian Cobra. Frequently, in those

A more-or-less traditional Indian snake charmer (photographed in Singapore) using a beautifully marked Indian Cobra, Naja naja. *Photo: K. H. Switak.*

The Egyptian Cobra, Naja haje*, was revered by the Egyptians. Photo: G. Dingerkus.*

ancient days, this Cobra was also used as a means of dispatching troublesome personalities without too much ado.

The species feeds on mice and rats and other small mammals. Generally speaking, the food animals are not devoured until they have died of the venomous bite.

Undoubtedly one of the best known exotic poisonous snakes is the Indian or Spectacled Cobra (*Naja naja*). Its native range extends from India southward and eastward via the Malay Archipelago to the Philippines. The famous spectacle pattern on the neck becomes visible when the snake expands its neck with the aid of the extended cervical ribs. At the same time, the cobra slowly sways from side to side with the now erect anterior part of the body and tries to bite the attacker. The subspecies *Naja naja kaouthia* normally only has a circle instead of the spectacle pattern.

All cobras can be very dangerous to human beings. The keeper of such snakes must take care, therefore, that the cages are securely closed, and any cleaning or other activities inside the terrarium must be handled with the greatest caution.

A number of *Naja* species fend off their enemies by spitting venom at them. In these snakes the opening of the venom groove is arranged in such a way that the poisonous secretion forced out under high muscular pressure is squirted out of the open mouth at right angles to the poison teeth and frequently hits the attacker in the eyes. A poisonous shower like that can cause blindness in

The speckled cobra of South Africa is Naja nivea. *All cobras should be considered deadly. Photo: C. Banks.*

human beings, too, unless the poison is rinsed off immediately.

Known for this behavior are the Black-necked Cobra (*Naja nigricollis*), which is common throughout tropical Africa, and the Ringhals (*Hemachatus haemachatus*).

Naja nivea lives in South Africa. This snake is of a light yellowish brown to sandy color and has a broad brown band on the front of the neck.

The largest cobra is the King Cobra or Hamadryad (*Ophiophagus hannah*) which attains the considerable length of over 4 m. It is native to India, Burma, southern China, Southeast Asia, and the Philippines. Keeping this snake in the terrarium is virtually impossible since it feeds almost exclusively on snakes. Substitute foods such as eels sometimes will be accepted, but force-feeding is the more common situation even in zoos.

The Hamadryad practices brood care and for the eggs builds a nest from dead leaves which is guarded by the female.

Southeast Asia and India

Naja oxiana *is a cobra of dry, cool steppes of southern Asia. Photo: S. Kochetov.*

are inhabited by several species of the genus *Bungarus*, the best known of these being the Banded Krait (*Bungarus fasciatus*), whose body is covered with very broad crossbands of black and yellow. In profile, the body of this species gives the curious impression of being triangular so that even well-nourished specimens of these moisture-loving elapids look starved.

Since they are extremely dangerous, it is not advisable to keep African mambas (genus *Dendroaspis*) in private dwellings. These snakes are lively, aggressive, big, and, rather like the tree snakes, frequent the the branches of average size trees. From there, they also attack or look out for their prey. Many adventurous accounts of the toxicity of Mambas have been given by travellers in their journals and it is indeed true that one bite is sufficient to kill a grown man within a few minutes, even where it has been possible to administer a specific serum. Well-known species are the Black Mamba (*Dendroaspis polylepis*) and the slightly smaller, tree-dwelling Western Green Mamba (*Dendroaspis viridis*).

The elapids in Australia and New Guinea have developed a particularly great wealth of different forms. Many of these species are as venomous as those from the Asian and African range. Common throughout southeastern Australia is the greatly feared and highly poisonous Eastern Tiger Snake (*Notechis scutatus*), an aggressive grayish elapid which is very prolific and produces up to 80 living young.

As opposed to the majority of Australian elapids which, like *Notechis scutatus* just mentioned, are livebearers, all species of the genus *Demansia* lay eggs. *Demansia psammophis*, which is a greenish brown above and light yellow on the underside, grows over 1 m long and lives in arid, stony terrain. Its venom is not dangerous to human beings. Even lizards stay alive for several minutes after sustaining the venomous bite.

The most colorful elapids are the coral snakes of the genus *Micrurus*. They survive for years in the terrarium. The latter must be equipped with a layer of earth, at least 15 cm deep, to enable these secretive snakes to burrow and hide. They can be fed on small lizards and young slowworms. Characteristic are the cylindrical body and the apparent absence of a neck.

In the southeastern United States is the Eastern

Notechis scutatus, *the Eastern Tiger Snake of Australia, has a well-deserved reputation as one of the most dangerous snakes on earth. Photo: S. Minton.*

Coral Snake (*Micrurus fulvius*). In *M. fulvius* the three colors—black, yellow, and red—are arranged in such a way that the black crossbands are bordered by the yellow rings.

The range of the *Micrurus* species starts in the southern region of the U.S.A and extends to northern Argentina. The largest species is *M. spixii*; it attains a length of over 1.5 m. The markings of this snake are unusual in that the rings are arranged in such a way that there are always three black ones very close together, separated only by narrow yellow bands. Between these black and yellow segments are broad cross bands of an intense red color.

Unless medical aid is received quickly, the venom of the coral snakes can also prove fatal to humans.

VIPERS
Viperidae

In the vipers the poison apparatus consists of two poison fangs, each with a closed poison canal, which are so long that they need to be folded back when the mouth is closed. They are not raised until the snake sinks them into the food animal's body.

The range of the vipers is restricted to the Old World. In the New World their place is occupied by the crotalids or pit vipers. These are venomous, too, and are distinguished from their close relatives, the viperids, by the presence of a special organ, the loreal pit organ, which helps them to perceive and track down their warm-blooded food.

The two most common European vipers are the Adder or Common European Viper *(Vipera berus)* and the Asp Viper *(Vipera aspis)*. The range of the Adder extends virtually over the whole of Europe as well as covering the northern region of Asia to as far as Japan. The coloration and markings

Micrurus dumerilii is a coral snake in which red rings touch black rings, unlike the species of the United States. Photo: R. S. Simmons.

vary, depending on locality and sex. The basic color can be anything from blue-gray, ash green, brownish gray, sand or straw yellow, light red, or blackish brown to jet black. The jet black animals without markings are described as "Hell's Adders" in Germany. On the head the Adder bears a characteristic X or) (pattern, and there is a zigzag line along the back, more blackish in male animals, brownish in females.

Adders favor the edges of forests and the clearings, terrain with plenty of bushes and shrubs, heather and moorland. The ground in their habitat is always slightly damp, never completely dry. They are very lethargic ground-dwelling animals and seldom climb. In an aquatic

The coral snake of the southern United States is the brightly colored but very dangerous *Micrurus fulvius. Photo: J. Iverson.*

The Common Viper or Adder of Europe is Vipera berus. The regular and complete plates on top of the head distinguish it from Vipera aspis. Photo: B. Kahl.

environment they become far more agile. In fact, when threatened they often seek refuge in the water.

In the spring, after emerging from hibernation, they hunt for food during the day, while turning into crepuscular or nocturnal animals during the warm summer months. The prey— mice, lizards, and frogs—are killed with a bite and not devoured until they have died. Like most viperids, *Vipera berus* is viviparous. Between mid-August and mid-September five to 18 young are born, measuring 14 to 21 cm in length. It is extremely interesting to watch the ritualized fights between the males which precede mating in April.

Not all Adders are suitable for the terrarium. This applies above all to wild catches. Even if caught uninjured they very often refuse all food. Young animals are easiest to acclimatize. The terrarium needs to be large and spacious; adequate ventilation and a water basin are essential. If the adders are to thrive in the terrarium, they must be kept warmer than the majority of snakes. Often a rise in temperature is all that is necessary to get fasting animals to take an interest in food.

The Asp Viper (*Vipera aspis*) is more common in the southwestern countries of Europe. Its coloration is no less variable than that of the Adder. The two species are about the same length as well. The average is about 60 cm, although female Adders often grow considerably longer than that. As opposed to the Adder, the Asp Viper favors dry scree slopes and disused quarries.

The smallest Viper found in central Europe is the Field Adder or Ursini's Viper (*Vipera ursinii*), which does not grow more than 50 cm long. Between the brown, wavy band on the back, usually situated on top of a lighter zone near the midline, and the lateral row of spots there is another row of smaller speckles. Although it occurs in the Viennese basin of Germany, in southern France, and in Italy, its main range, however, is the Balkan countries. As the common name suggests, this snake favors heaths and meadows as well as treeless grassland. *Vipera ursinii* is slow to bite and far more suitable for the terrarium than the Adder and the Asp Viper, since it readily accepts its food. The latter consists of mice, lizards, and frogs. Birds' eggs are also eaten from time to time.

Lataste's Viper (*Vipera latasti*), native to Spain and North Africa, has either a mound-like projection or a small horn on the tip of its snout. In its basic color this viper is similar to the Adder; the dark dorsal band is composed of lozenge-shaped, elliptical, or circular patches. Even more distinct is the horn of the Sand or Horned Viper (*Vipera ammodytes*). This horn consists of a fleshy, soft projection covered with scales.

The Sand Viper attains a maximum length of 95 cm and is thus the largest venomous snake of central Europe. It is common in southeastern Europe. Its

Vipera ursinii, the Field Adder, is the smallest viper of central Europe. Because it adapts well to captivity and feeds well, it often is kept in terraria. Photo: S. Kochetov.

One of the more poorly known vipers of the Middle East is the Ottoman Viper, Vipera xanthina. *It is one of the larger species of the genus. Photo: B. Kahl.*

prey are mice, moles, birds, and sometimes lizards as well. This magnificent viper can grow very old in captivity, readily accepts its food, and is less in need of warmth than are *Vipera ursinii* and *Vipera aspis*.

Three large vipers—1.5 m and more—live in southeastern Europe, in the adjoining region of Asia Minor, and in North Africa. The Ottoman Viper (*Vipera xanthina*) occurs in southwestern Asia; it is absent from Syria and Palestine. Closely related to it is the Blunt-nosed or Levant Viper (*Vipera lebetina*), which needs higher temperatures. Except for Egypt, this species is distributed all over North

The Plain Puff Adder, Bitis inornata, *from southern Africa. Photo: K. H. Switak.*

Facing page: Top: Unechis nigrostriatus, *a small elapid from Australia. Photo: K. H. Switak.* **Bottom:** *Russell's Viper,* Vipera russellii, *may be the snake that causes more human fatalities each year than any other single species. Photo: S. Kochetov.*

Africa. It occurs from Turkey via Arabia to Russia, in India and the Caucasus. Southern Libya, Jordan, and Israel are the home of *Vipera palaestinae.*

In the North African deserts lives the strange looking Horned Viper, *Cerastes cerastes.* A conspicuous characteristic of this sand-colored species with brown spots and a maximum length of 75 cm is a pointed scaly process above each eye. These snakes like to bury themselves in the hot sand. They burrow very rapidly, making sidewinding movements with the body and using the ventral scales to assist them. Small heaps of sand serve as camouflage. It is essential, therefore, to put a layer of sand, at least 12 cm deep, into the terrarium and to provide

Causus maculatus, *a night adder from Africa. Photo: C. Banks.*

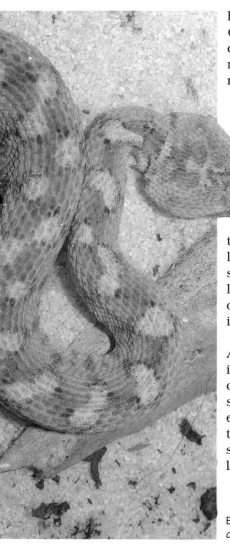

heating at that level. *Cerastes cerastes* is crepuscular and feeds mostly on birds in its natural environment.

Russell's Viper (*Vipera russellii*), whose range extends from India to Taiwan, possesses a lively color pattern of reddish brown blotches with white and black edges arranged on the back in three longitudinal rows. This species, which attains a length of up to 1.7 m, is one of the most feared snakes in its native range.

Mole vipers of the genus *Atractaspis* are very seldom imported and kept. These cylindrical snakes lead a subterranean, burrowing existence. The narrow head, the small eyes, and the short tail indicate they have largely adapted to a life

Echis coloratus, a desert-dwelling carpet viper. Photo: J. T. Kellnhauser.

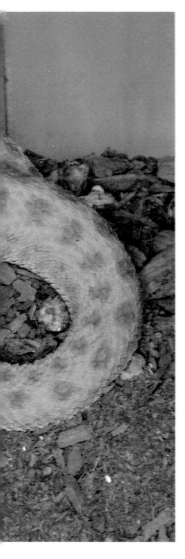

The genus Cerastes *contains species adapted to extreme desert conditions.* **Above** *is the Horned Viper or African Sidewinder,* Cerastes cerastes*;* **to the left** *is* Cerastes vipera, *the Sahara Sand Viper. Photos:* **Above:** *C. Banks;* **Left:** *S. Minton.*

underground.

Not often imported either are the Night Adders of the genus *Causus*. They are true ground-dwelling snakes and live in the regions south of the Sahara. The genus *Causus* is comprised of four species, among which *Causus rhombeatus* and *Causus resimus* possess very strongly developed poison glands. The latter extend beyond the region of the head to the anterior third of the body. The diet of these vipers, which grow to an average length of 60 cm, curiously enough consists of toads and frogs. *Causus* species are oviparous.

The Carpet or Saw-scaled Viper, *Echis carinatus*, is said to possess the most effective viperine poison of all. This snake, which grows to about 70 cm in length, occurs from northern Africa via western Asia to India and Sri Lanka. When excited it arranges itself into a kind of figure 8 and rubs the keeled scales of its flanks together. The rubbing of the rough scales on alternate sides produces a rustling and hissing noise. The Carpet Viper is extremely irascible and quick and eager to bite, and its effective poison makes it one of the most dangerous of all the venomous snakes. The novice is therefore urged to refrain from keeping this species.

The genus *Bitis* includes a number of vipers which are characteristic of Africa. In size they range from the giant Gabon Viper (*Bitis gabonica*), which reaches a length of up to 2 m, to the 30 cm long *Bitis peringueyi*.

The most common species, with the widest range of distribution, is the Puff Adder (*Bitis arietans*) which is adorned with semi-lunar yellow to black angular patches on the brown to gray background color of the back. It occurs all over the African continent as far south as the Cape of Good Hope, with

Some Gaboon Vipers have a horn on the snout similar to those of the Rhinoceros Viper. This form or subspecies is Bitis gabonica rhinoceros. *Photo: R. T. Zappalorti.*

the exception of the northern coastal zone and the tropical rain forest. Its diet consists of smaller rodents up to the size of a rat. *Bitis arietans* and other species have been successfully bred in the terrarium on a number of occasions. An adult female can produce up to 60 young which measure 19 to 20 cm at the time of birth.

Larger than *Bitis arietans* is the Gaboon Viper (*Bitis gabonica*). Its native range is tropical equatorial Africa. The upper parts are of a light reddish brown color as a rule, with a variable dorsal pattern of dark triangles and squares.

Bitis gabonica rhinoceros is a subspecies of the Gaboon Viper which has horns on the snout. It occurs in Liberia and on the Gold Coast.

Even more magnificent in color than the Gaboon Viper is the Rhinoceros Viper (*Bitis nasicornis*). It inhabits the tropical rain forests of Africa and is one of the most beautiful viperids. The back is purple and blue in color, and the flanks are adorned with green triangles with black and deep blue edges. This species remains smaller than *Bitis gabonica*, its average length being about 1.2 m, and it owes its popular name to the large scaly horns at the anterior end of the snout which look pointed when raised.

More suitable for the

A true Rhinoceros Viper, Bitis nasicornis*, has a broad dark arrow on the head rather than a narrow dark line as in the Gaboon Viper. Photo: K. Lucas.*

Head study of Bitis peringueyi, *a small desert-dwelling puff adder. Note the dorsally directed eyes. Photo: K. H. Switak.*

hobbyist than the large and delicate *Bitis* species are the smaller, hardier species: the Horned Adder (*Bitis caudalis*) which grows to only 40 cm in length, *Bitis cornuta*, and the very small *Bitis peringueyi* which, like *Cerastes cerastes*, is able to bury itself in the sand within a few minutes.

PIT VIPERS
Crotalidae

Because the crotalids and viperids are so closely related, these two groups of snakes, now ranked as independent families, were for a long time classified jointly as the family Viperidae.

Their "pit organ," which all of them possess, has made the crotalids a particularly successful group of snakes in the New World. Among them are not only tree-dwelling snakes with a characteristic prehensile tail, but also forms that have conquered the water as their habitat.

The function of the pit organ was already pointed out in the chapter on viperids. Purely externally, and on both sides, there is visible an opening between the nostril and the eye. Inside the cavity this is covered by a slightly sunken membrane by means of which the entire cavity is divided into an external and internal pit. A large quantity of free nerve endings terminate in the membrane. The former are supplied by a tactile nerve. Appropriate experiments have established beyond doubt that the pit organ has the function of temperature perception and detects air movement at the same time. It is not surprising, therefore, that nocturnal pit vipers locate and seize warm-blooded prey with unbelievable accuracy.

The Water Moccasin or Cottonmouth (*Agkistrodon piscivorus*) is native to the southeastern states of the U.S.A. Southward, its range extends to the mouth of the Rio Grande del Norte. The color of the adult animals is a uniform dark brown or black. They attain a length of 1.6 m. Immature animals bear crossbands and possess a yellow tip to the tail which they move to and fro like a pendulum as though trying to bait their prey with it. In the

A Water Moccasin, Agkistrodon piscivorus. *This is one of the most common—and respected—venomous snakes of southern United States. Large specimens can cause human deaths. Photo: R. T. Zappalorti.*

terrarium the Cottonmouth is hardy and resistant. There has been a report of a pair having been kept for over 11 years. Breeding attempts in captivity have also been successful on a number of occasions; the female gives birth to five to 15 living young. *Agkistrodon*

Two baby Water Moccasins. Notice the yellow tail tip, which is used to lure in curious lizards and other prey. The tip darkens with age. Photo: W. B. Allen, Jr.

piscivorous does not live solely on fish, as the specific name seems to suggest, but also feeds on mammals, birds, and lizards.

The more colorful Cantil or Mexican Moccasin (*Agkistrodon bilineatus*) is found in Mexico.

The Copperhead (*Agkistrodon contortrix*) exists in several different subspecies. The nominate form, *Agkistrodon contortrix contortrix*, inhabits the coastal regions of the Atlantic and of the Gulf of Mexico; *Agkistrodon contortrix mokeson* is distributed from southern New England via New York and Pennsylvania to the middle West. *Agkistrodon contortrix laticinctus* inhabits the regions between Texas and northern Kansas. In this subspecies the reddish brown bands characteristic for all races are very broad. The fourth, lesser known, form is *Agkistrodon contortrix pictigaster*, which is clearly distinguished from the others by the dark blotches on its underside and occurs in Texas as well as in northern Mexico.

The Copperheads favor broadleafed woods and terrain with plenty of bushes. They feed predominantly on smaller mammals and lizards. Very often they also devour larger insects and their larvae, especially locusts.

Species of the genus *Agkistrodon* also occur in the Old World. One such species is *Agkistrodon halys*, native to the steppes of southeastern Russia, although in the form of several geographical races it extends over central Asia to Japan. The light gray to light brownish gray snake with its pattern of dark crossbands attains an average length of 60 cm. It

Facing page: A Northern Copperhead, Agkistrodon contortrix mokasen. Photo: R. T. Zappalorti. *Below:* Agkistrodon blomhoffi, one of several species of Asian copperheads found in Russia, China, and Japan. Photo: S. Kochetov.

Crotalus viridis concolor, *a nearly unicolor subspecies of the Prairie Rattlesnake. Photo: J. Wines.*

feeds on mice and young birds and is not as dependent on warmth as many species from the New World tend to be.

Most people are familiar with the Rattlesnakes, which also belong to the

Rattlesnakes vary greatly in size. The Timber Rattlesnake, Crotalus horridus, *(below) may reach almost 2 meters in length and is very bulky, while the Pigmy Rattlesnake,* Sistrurus miliarius, *(facing page) seldom exceeds half a meter. Photos:* **Below:** *R. T. Zappalorti;* **Facing page:** *R. Everhart.*

An albino Western Diamondback Rattlesnake,
Crotalus atrox. *Photo: R. Everhart.*

crotalids. These animals owe their distinguishing name to the strange rattle on the tail which consists of several segments or cones. The cones are hard and dry and are really nothing more than the remnants of cast skin. Newly born snakes have only a knob or "button" at the tip of the tail. It has a ring-shaped constriction which holds the next rattle in place when the rest of the skin is shed. With each successive molt another segment is added to the rattle. Older animals no longer have the complete set of segments, however. A greater or lesser number of these is lost in the course of time. The famous whirring noise is produced when the tail is raised and the rattle is moved. The noise is thought to be a warning signal for larger animals in the same habitat.

The pygmy rattlesnakes (genus *Sistrurus*) have a very small rattle. Only the Massasauga (*Sistrurus catenatus*) and the Pygmy Rattlesnake (*Sistrurus miliarius*) shall be mentioned here. They are native to the central and southern sections of the United States. The former favors swampy, damp more northern terrain, while *Sistrurus miliarius* often is found more in a drier environment.

The biggest rattlesnake and hence the largest poisonous snake in North America is the Eastern Diamondback Rattlesnake (*Crotalus adamanteus*). It grows over 2.5 m long and on a brownish olive background has a pattern of black to blackish brown spots with yellow borders.
The Western Diamondback (*Crotalus atrox*), with a maximum length of 2.1 m, is the

The Timber Rattlesnake of the eastern United States is very variable in color and pattern. Very dark individuals are not uncommon. Photo: R. Everhart.

second largest member of its genus. It occurs among the mesquite shrubs and dense stands of cacti in the desert-like plains and hilly terrain of western North America.

The Timber Rattlesnake *(Crotalus horridus)* grows to almost 2 m in length. Of the Prairie Rattlesnake *(Crotalus viridus)* several geographical races are found on grassy

Although the Timber Rattlesnake once was common over much of the eastern United States, like other venomous snakes it has been killed whenever found. Additionally, its habitat has been destroyed or modified. Photo: R. Everhart.

terrain in western North America.

One of the smallest rattlesnake is the Sidewinder (*Crotalus cerastes*), which grows to a

The Sidewinder, Crotalus cerastes, *and its distinctive tracks. Photo: K. H. Switak.*

mere 60 cm in length. It owes its Latin name to the horn-like enlargement of its e y e b r o w scales.

Crotalids from the Old World are mostly species of the genus *Trimeresurus*. They occur from China and Formosa to Sri Lanka and are also represented in the Indo-Australian range by a few tree-dwelling species.

One such arboreal snake is *Trimeresurus wagleri*. These fat, green animals with yellow crossbands hang on to the branches by a prehensile tail. The triangular head is carried by a thin neck and markedly contrasts with the body.

Trimeresurus albolabris hails from tropical southern Asia and the Malay Archipelago. This is another arboreal snake. Well camouflaged by its leaf green color and red prehensile tail, it lurks among dense foliage, waiting

Trimeresurus trigonocephalus *is one of many species of Asian pit vipers that closely resemble the American snakes of the genus* Bothrops. *Photo: S. Kochetov.*

for prey.

Trimeresurus monticola, on the other hand, is a ground-dwelling species. The females practice brood care. The eggs, laid among piles of bamboo or leaves, are carefully guarded and fiercely defended against enemies.

Species of the New World genus *Bothrops* are common in Central and South America. In many the conspicuous color pattern consists of pale, lozenge-shaped blotches with black edges on a brown or brownish gray background. If the full amount of poison is injected with a bite, a large species can kill a human being within a few minutes. Extensive bleeding in the musculature marks the victim of a *Bothrops* bite. Anyone who keeps these snakes must deposit a specific serum with his doctor or ensure that it is stocked by the nearest pharmacist.

Very common in Brazil is *Bothrops jararaca*, an olive-brown snake with dark spots which, like nearly all *Bothrops* species, feeds on birds and rodents.

Bothrops schlegeli of Central America and northwestern South America is a bluish green snake with red spots that spends the day resting on climbing branches, always securely anchored by its purplish red prehensile tail.

One of the biggest pit vipers is the Bushmaster (*Lachesis muta*), which reaches a maximum length of 4 m. It occurs in the countries from southern Central America to Brazil, Peru, and Bolivia. This species is not suitable for the terrarium. The Bushmaster is very delicate and often refuses all food over very long periods.

Above: A bright yellow color phase of the Eyelash Tree Viper, Bothrops schlegeli of Central America. This is one of the mostly commonly kept venomous snakes. Photo: A. Kerstitch. *Below:* The bright green Trimeresurus stejnegeri *is only one of several species of similar-appearing arboreal species of the genus from southern Asia. Photo: R. E. Kuntz.*

SUGGESTED READING

ATLAS OF SNAKES OF THE WORLD
by J. Coborn
TFH TS-128
Almost 600 pages, over 1,200 full-color photos
A survey of the full variety of snakes, natural history and much more!

KINGSNAKES AND MILK SNAKES
by R. Markel
TFH TS-125
6 x 9", 160 pages, over 150 photos
Detailed coverage of all the species of kingsnakes and milk snakes. Special sections on feeding, breeding, and husbandry.

PYTHONS AND BOAS
by P. Stafford
TFH PS-846
5 $^1/_2$ x 8", 198 pages, over 190 photos
An impressive book for the owners of pythons or boas.

REPTILE DISEASES
by R. Hackbarth
TFH KW-197
5 $^1/2$ x 8 $^1/2$", 96 pages, fully illustrated
The ultimate book of reptile health and treatment of disease.

ENCYCLOPEDIA OF REPTILES AND AMPHIBIANS
by J. Breen
TFH H-935
5 $^1/2$ x 8", 576 pages, over 550 photos
Offers enormous coverage of the care, collection, and identification of reptiles and amphibians.

THE COMPLETELY ILLUSTRATED ATLAS OF REPTILES AND AMPHIBIANS FOR THE TERRARIUM
by F. Obst, et al
TFH H-1102
8 $^1/4$ x 12 $^1/4$", 830 pages, over 2000 photos
The most comprehensive and beautiful volume of reptiles and amphibians for the terrarium, plus oddballs and rarities, that any hobbyist or scientist is likely to ever encounter.